WWJD the question that will change your life

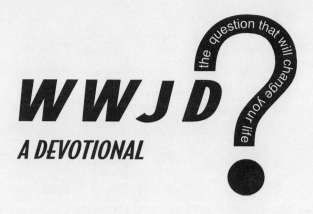

W W J D ?

the question that will change your life

A DEVOTIONAL

BEVERLY COURREGE
PAUL MEIER, M.D.
HEIDI GARDINER

A
JANET
THOMA
BOOK

THOMAS NELSON PUBLISHERS
Nashville

Published in Nashville, Tennessee, by Thomas Nelson, Inc., Publishers.

The Bible version used in this publication is THE NEW KING JAMES
VERSION. Copyright © 1979, 1980, 1982, 1990, Thomas Nelson, Inc.,
Publishers.

Library of Congress Cataloging-in-Publication Data
Meier, Paul D.
    WWJD? : the question that will change your life : a devotional / Paul
Meier, Beverly Courrege, Heidi Gardiner.
        p.   cm.
    ISBN 0-7852-7521-5 (hardcover)
    1. Jesus—Example—Prayer-books and devotions—English.
I. Courrege, Beverly. II. Gardiner, Heidi. III. Title.
BT304.2.M45   1998
242—dc21   98-21709
                                                                CIP

Printed in the United States of America.
1 2 3 4 5 6 BVG 03 02 01 00 99 98

To my sister, Charmaine Bode, and her husband, Todd, and sons, Shawn and Wesley.

To my brother, Barry Beasley, and to the memory of our parents, Gabriel and Sunshine.

To the memory of my husband's parents, George and Mary.

To my brother and sister-in-law, David and Helen Courrege, and their children, J. D. and Natasha.

To my husband, Boo, and our son, Cord, and daughter, J. J.

Your lives enrich mine, and the greatest desire of my heart is for our families to spend God's eternity together.
—Beverly Courrege

For my husband, John—
Freely . . .
Faithfully . . .
Forever . . .
—Heidi Gardiner

CONTENTS

CONTENTS

CONTENTS

ACKNOWLEDGMENTS

To Bob James and his wife, Kelli. I owe an eternal debt of gratitude for your integrity, vision, and editing of my first book with Honor Books that opened the door to my writing career.

Special thanks to Paul Meier for asking me to share in this writing project and introducing me to Janet Thoma, our editor.

Thank you, Janet, for helping me become the writer I long to be. You have become a dear friend and mentor whose guidance I will never cease to seek.

And to Todd Ross, our managing editor at Janet Thoma Books, a division of Thomas Nelson Publishers. As technically challenged as I am, you managed to teach me how to e-mail my manuscripts and reach editing deadlines within cyberseconds!

Thank you, Thomas Nelson Publishers, for allowing me the privilege of becoming one of your authors. Everyone on your staff who I have worked with has been so generous with their time, advice, and expertise, always reflecting the higher standards a Christian publishing house purposes to be.

And Heidi Johnson Gardiner, our coauthor for this book, talented singer, songwriter, and friend. I'm so proud of you. So young and so gifted!

— Beverly Courrege

I am very grateful to Beverly and Paul, my coauthors and friends. Thank you for your insight and encouragement. It is truly an honor to have conspired with you both on this project. Many thanks to Janet Thoma and Thomas Nelson Publishers for giving me the chance to share what's in my heart.

I want to extend a special note of appreciation to my husband, John; my mom and dad; my brother, Dwight, and his wife, Vicki; the Windsors, and the many friends who have contributed the stories of their lives that have greatly enriched mine. Thank you.

— Heidi Gardiner

INTRODUCTION

In 1897 Charles Sheldon wrote a book, *In His Steps*, where a fictional church congregation asked themselves the question *What would Jesus do?* regarding many everyday circumstances. For generations since the publication of that book, many Christian children have grown up in homes where the parents posed this question to them as a means of developing a moral sense.

Sensing the need for an updated look at the question, Sheldon's grandson wrote another *What would Jesus do?* novel for the nineties. In the last two years, the question *What would Jesus do?* has seen a resurgence in the church and has become quite a phenomenon. Shortened to WWJD?, this question is found on bracelets, T-shirts, Bible covers, ball caps, engraved rocks, wall plaques, memo pads, and all sorts of other personal accessories. These items are meant to be used as a prompt to remind the bearer to ask that question when facing challenging circumstances.

In this book, *WWJD? The Question That Will Change Your Life*, we three authors have decided to share with you the very personal and very practical ways we have used *WWJD?* and times when we should have used *WWJD?* but didn't. These devotions will present you with Scripture that speaks to the issue at hand, insight about how Jesus would resolve the situation, and some thoughts on which to meditate throughout your day or week.

The question *What would Jesus do?* really stands for several questions: *What would Jesus say?*, *What would Jesus have me do?*, and *What principles did Jesus model that I can apply to this situation?* You'll see that we three, as imperfect humans, have gotten ourselves in messes Jesus never would have, so the exact question of *WWJD?* doesn't exactly fit. But we believe that *WWJD?* is more than one question, it is an attitude. Daily choosing to walk in the will and example of Christ Jesus is *WWJD?*. Simply put, *WWJD?* is nothing more than living Christianly. But the discipline and action of asking the question each time we are faced with a difficult situation is what wearing the bracelet or ball cap is all about.

We hope that you will be blessed, challenged, and encouraged as you read our personal experiences. These pages should give you insight into how you can use *WWJD?* as a tool to grow in your walk with Jesus and let your light shine throughout the world.

You've Come a Long Way, Baby

No temptation has overtaken you except such as is common to man; but God is faithful, who will not allow you to be tempted beyond what you are able, but with the temptation will also make the way of escape, that you may be able to bear it. (1 Cor. 10:13)

I'm an ex smoker, if there really is such a thing. When I was eighteen years old, smoking was not only socially acceptable, but the most glamorous girls from the pages of fashion magazines appeared even more so with a long "elegant" cigarette between their perfectly painted lips. Add to that two smoking parents—how could a girl resist?

In my mid-twenties, as my walk with the Lord became significant, I realized smoking was definitely something God did not want me to do. How did I know? I felt His displeasure every time I lit up. So, why didn't God miraculously deliver me from the nicotine demon?

In my late thirties I was between one of the five times I

had tried to quit smoking. Oh! Did I mention I was a closet smoker? No one in my life knew I was still puffing. My husband was suspicious, and my kids had caught me in the back yard lighting up a few times, but none of my friends at church had a clue.

One day I was in the grocery store checkout line when my dear friend Linda, who was attending a Bible study *I was teaching*, stepped in line behind me. In my cart was a package of cigarettes.

How stupid of me. I usually went to remote service stations to purchase my stash. I'm not even sure she initially saw the cigarettes. My heart was pounding and my mind spinning as I tried to think of a plausible explanation. Well, Jesus would not have done what I did next. I lied. I actually told her I was buying the cigarettes for a friend! In my head I rationalized that I did actually have a smoking friend who probably would smoke a couple of cigarettes from this pack. Oh, yes! My smoking friends were very helpful in keeping my secret. I don't remember the rest of our conversation, but I am sure we mentioned seeing each other at our next Bible study. What had I done?

At that point only God and I knew I had lied. And do you know what? That was enough! I was miserable. Smoking became insignificant compared to my blatant lie.

Well, Jesus, God the Father, and the Holy Spirit wouldn't let it go! During the next twenty-four hours I thought of nothing else. I couldn't even sleep that night. The next morning I knew I had to do something and so I prayed for God's wisdom.

First, I tried just confessing to my husband. Of course he was disappointed in my smoking, but he still loved me. Just telling him didn't help the battle that was warring inside me because of the lie, however. In fact, the stress of the situation made me want another cigarette!

Still convicted, I went to see Linda. I knew I had to tell her everything. As I approached her front door, another dear friend was just leaving her house and was pleasantly surprised to see me. Startled and overcome by guilt, I blurted out the whole story to her and asked her to come back inside Linda's house while I confessed yet another time.

How could I possibly want another cigarette with all the turmoil it was causing me? But at that moment I did. I confessed with my mouth to Linda and Christy what had transpired in the last twenty-four hours and stated that I really didn't want to smoke. They assured me they didn't love me any less for either the smoking or the lie.

What would Jesus do? Jesus was truth incarnate, no lie would ever come from His lips nor would a cigarette ever touch them. But Jesus was tempted, He understood the pull of the flesh, and He also understood the complexities of human relationships and forgiveness. Considering the poor choices I had already made and the mess I was in, Jesus surely would have me confess the truth to my friends and ask them to pray for the circumstance and trust God to work for good in my life.

That morning, my friends fervently prayed with and for me,

and I felt the lifting of a heavy burden. The unwelcome need for cigarettes gradually left me and within a few months I was at last an ex smoker.

White lies and little lies are destructive in ways you cannot imagine. Remember to follow Jesus' example and speak the truth. But if you slip, take heart in God's promise to provide "a way of escape" and search for a just solution—be it telling the truth or making amends—that is honoring to God.

—BC

Specks
and Planks

*And why do you look at the speck in your brother's eye,
but do not consider the plank in your own eye? Or how
can you say to your brother, "Let me remove the speck
from your eye"; and look, a plank is in your own eye?
Hypocrite! First remove the plank from your own eye, and
then you will see clearly to remove the speck from your
brother's eye. (Matt. 7:3–5)*

I am a psychiatrist. As a member of this profession of people helpers, I problem solve difficult family situations, do
a lot of listening and empathizing, and dispense a lot of
advice. You'd think I'd easily be able to spot and solve problems in my own family. Unfortunately, several years ago when
our youngest daughter was fourteen, she sank into a clinical
depression and ran away from home. When she came back to
us, she decided to seek help from a pastoral counselor who
had no affiliation with me whatsoever.

Simply glad to have her home, I thanked God she was

safe and seeing a Christian counselor. As I thought about our situation, I reasoned that there were three factors that determine how each of our children turn out: genes, environment, and personal choices. Having a Christian psychiatrist for a father and a marriage and family therapist for a mother, her genes and environment *certainly couldn't* have caused her problems, so *she* must have been making some lousy choices that led to her depression. I assumed that her counselor would help her straighten out *her* bad choices.

To my surprise and chagrin, her counselor called me on the phone one day and said, "Dr. Meier, I think I've figured out what *you* are doing wrong that is contributing to your daughter's depression. Can you and your wife join your daughter and me for a family session on Saturday?"

I told him "I'd love to come!" but that was not really the truth. I was stunned and insulted. After all, I have written fifty books about psychiatry including several on raising children. How could I have done anything wrong? What would I say to the counselor? If I agreed with him that I was doing something wrong, I would be lying because I honestly didn't see any way I could be at fault. But if I denied making mistakes as a father, he would think I was defensive and I certainly wouldn't want anyone to think Paul Meier was defensive!

On the night before the family session, still undecided about what to say to my daughter's counselor, God woke me up with a terrible dream. Jesus was in the dream leaning over me and saying again and again in a deep voice, "Matthew seven, verses three through five." I woke up and snuck out of bed so I wouldn't wake my wife. I went in the next room to look up the verses given to me in my dream. The verses convicted me of being a hypocrite and seeing only the tiny speck in my daughter's eye instead of the lumbering log in my own. I suddenly realized that I had been too picky and critical of her for quite some time. I believe she reminded me, at an unconscious level, of my own faults. I wept, apologized to God, went back to sleep, and told no one about the dream, not even my wife.

At the family session a few hours later, the counselor pulled a Bible out from his desk, opened it up, and began reading. Guess what he read? Matthew 7:3–5. I immediately recognized this as a message from God and began weeping again. I shared my dream and my realization to my daughter. During the next months we worked hard to repair the damage done, and now, I'm proud to say, we are good friends. At that time in my life I didn't often ask, *What would Jesus do?* But in my dream, Jesus gave me a clear sign of how I should begin to repair my relationship with my daughter.

Throughout this episode I should have asked WWJD? There are many things I wished I had handled differently, not the least of which is

*everything that led to my daughter's running
away in the first place. But God is faithful.
When He knew I would have no choice but to
listen, God told me what He wanted me to do.
Even now, asking WWJD?, I believe Jesus wants
me to confess this sin of pride and criticism
publicly to encourage other parents to examine
their own influences, positive and negative, on
their children and to work to improve these
cherished relationships. All of us see specks and
miss logs from time to time. One of the insidious
things about arrogance is that it is so difficult to
recognize in oneself, especially when it is
cloaked under the good intentions of parenting.*

*Jesus took on the mantle of humility even
though He was always right. Without that
infallibility ourselves, maintaining an open
mind and uncritical heart will go a long way
toward avoiding hypocrisy in our own homes
and following God's wise and imperative
advice.*

—PM

Precious
Moments

Let the little children come to Me, and do not forbid
them; for of such is the kingdom of God . . . And He took
them up in His arms, laid His hands on them, and
blessed them. (Mark 10:14b,16)

I am one of those fortunate children who grew up in a household with a stay-at-home mom. Doubly fortunate for me and my brother, my father was self-employed and always made his own schedule. Consequently, my parents spent a great deal of time with us and constantly took us on trips or fun adventures. My dad even took me with him when he was making sales calls.

Over the years, we did a lot of traveling together. Every winter we went skiing in Colorado and then we would trek back again in the summer for hiking and camping. We took trips to Germany to visit my mom's relatives, which enabled us to travel through Europe several times.

My most treasured memories, however, come from all our

camping adventures. When I was five years old, my family got involved in cross-country motorcycling. Almost every other weekend, Mom and Dad would load up the car, hitch on the motorcycle trailer, and off we would go to the Flying "P" Ranch in Weatherford, Texas. Several other family friends from our church also got involved.

We had so much fun! There were big bonfires at night with singing and laughter, and during the day we enjoyed hundreds of miles of trails winding through creek bottoms, woods, and lake shores. Under the hot sun we swam in the lakes, and at night we cooled down on Baldy peak, the highest spot on the ranch, and lay back to count shooting stars. This was where I learned to appreciate the many blessings in life given by God. But the Flying "P" was much more than that.

During that decade of adventure, Mom and Dad used the Flying "P" to develop a close, lifelong bond within our family. They gave us the most treasured thing parents can give to children—time. Those weekends were an escape from the city and the peer pressure kids face day in and day out. By being involved in our lives through those years, our parents demonstrated their constant love for us, the stability of their marriage, and that we could always rely on them. This strength and commitment to family kept us from looking for acceptance in all the wrong places.

Concerning parenting, I don't think my parents ever explicitly asked themselves, *What would Jesus do?*, but they had many choices to make where Jesus' influence would be evident, including how they spent their time. My heart aches when I hear about families who are too busy to sit down for a meal together or are so consumed with activities, job pressures, and social obligations that they won't even take a little time to just goof off together and build memories. My parents modeled Jesus' love by opening their arms, accepting us, and giving us themselves. Should the Lord bless my husband and me with the tremendous honor of raising children, I hope to emulate the commitment and love shown to me and my brother at the Flying "P".

Remember where your eternal investments are. They don't just impact the moment, they impact a lifetime. The next time your children are underfoot and you feel like you really have something more important to do, just ask yourself, WWJD?

—HG

First Come, First Served

*The LORD your God has been with you; you have lacked
nothing. (Deut. 2:7c)*

Two days after consenting to write some personal applications of the *What would Jesus do?* principle, I was
thoroughly confronted and convicted by the question's
power.

You see, I'm prone to anxiety attacks in large crowds. The
Lord miraculously carries me through my talks with women's
groups, but I consciously avoid all malls. You can imagine
how happy this makes my husband!

The auditorium hosting my nephew's graduation from
college has a capacity seating for 2,398 people including the
graduates! If there are 500 graduates and seating is first come,
first served then there are only 3.8 seats for each student's family members. I am sure you see where I am going with this—
there were not enough seats!

My husband and I arrived so early that we were at the front

entrance to the auditorium floor waiting to secure the ten seats we needed. The foyer behind us filled so rapidly it indicated that the crowd would certainly be beyond capacity.

When the door opened, allowing people to enter one by one, I was severed from my husband's arm by the push of humanity, wanting their up close and personal seating for the ceremony. Always resourceful, my husband was able to secure an entire row of ten seats. Eventually the throng of people moved me toward my husband's beckoning wave and he posted me on the main aisle, first chair.

Immediately I was questioned by other attendees because I was saving a whole row. After several such episodes I was feeling a little anxious so I asked my husband to switch places with me. His first challenge came from a rather robust woman in stature and in nature. She pushed my husband aside and loudly declared, "You can't save the whole row. I'm going to sit here!" then barreled toward me and pushed me aside too! By then, the crowd was so thick I had to very ungracefully crawl over her and her husband to take the seat next to them. It wasn't until after an intense verbal exchange that my husband finally conceded three seats to them.

His next challenge was with a Cruella DeVille (remember *101 Dalmatians*?). This woman was even more vehement than the first as she accosted my husband. This was really challenging our *WWJD?* thinking. I had a feeling that if the second woman had been a man, my husband might have actually punched her out. I really couldn't believe how bad it got! By the time the rest of our family arrived we only had five seats left. I was "smiling" through my teeth at the second woman, trying not to hyperventilate or cry to give her the satisfaction of victory. I took some deep breaths, and wiped away some errant tears as I walked away from the madness with my sanctification askew. Five of us took our seats on the third floor balcony with a pirate's perch view of center stage only. After we watched my nephew walk across the stage and receive his diploma, my husband and I left. Our early exit was ill-mannered too!

Later, I thought about the stories of the different multitudes in the Bible, especially the multitude of more than five thousand people that Jesus fed. *Jesus* knew they were all going to eat. Do you imagine there were some people in that crowd who were worried there would only be bread and no fish left by the time it got to them, if they got to eat at all? Perhaps they pushed their way to the head of the line, tried to hoard food for their friends, or hurled verbal unpleasantries to others waiting for their share. Or do you think someone complained about how long they had to wait for food because there was only one basket? Everyone gathered at the event with an expectant heart, but some didn't understand that it wasn't necessary to take aggressive, unpleasant action to be first or receive the best.

I'm not sure if it was my general anxiety about the situation or a "crowd mentality" that took over at my nephew's graduation, but my husband and I fell short of the mark for acceptable behavior. Maybe we should have had a neon sign with

WWJD? in front of us instead of a bracelet. But reflecting on the day has helped us to remember Jesus and how He would have us act in just such a stressful situation.

There are two applications of WWJD? here. First, in our bearing and actions we are always representatives of Christ and should be asking WWJD? whenever difficult situations arise or when confronted with difficult people. Second, we are to trust Jesus and His bountiful provision for us throughout life. Jesus does not want us to become anxious or act on "first come, first served." He intends to provide what we truly need even when we are not sure what that should be ourselves.

—BC

LEGACY OF
FAITHFULNESS

How beautiful are the feet of those who preach the
gospel of peace,
Who bring glad tidings of good things!
(Rom. 10:15b)

Following God's direction in choices today can have implications for many generations. Consider the remarkable faithfulness of two German shoe repairmen who sought God's direction for their lives and went on a unique mission trip. They traveled to a German town along the Volga river in far-away Russia, and went door-to-door mending soles and winning souls.

When not practicing their trade these two men held Bible studies and shared the gospel at every opportunity. Within a year they were gone and never heard from again, but because of their Bible studies and witnessing, the town of about eight thousand was never the same. About a third of the townspeople became believers in Jesus, including two separate families of Meiers. The Meiers were so devout, several became pastors and, to this very day, nearly all of their descendants are still committed believers in Jesus.

In 1917, the communist revolution took place in Russia and the Red Army went to the town of my ancestors, drafting them into the army. Those who refused were taken in front of their homes and shot to death. My parents were both about eight years old at the time and were friends, even though my mother was poor and my father was rich. My paternal grandfather was a wealthy factory owner and even had separate quarters behind his home for their more than thirty servants.

When the Red Army came to my father's home, they took my father's pony, shot some of his uncles, and took over his house as their headquarters. My mother's and father's families fled and escaped with nothing, first to St. Petersburg, where they nearly starved to death, then to Germany, and finally, by the time they were teenagers, to America. In their twenties, my parents were reunited in Kansas and soon fell in love, got married, went to Michigan on their honeymoon and decided to move there.

Because of the heritage passed on to them through the faithfulness of the two cobblers and through the continued faithfulness and conscious choices of other generations of Meiers, my mother and father were totally devoted to Christ, frequent soulwinners, and active churchgoers. We were financially poor (my dad a carpenter, my mom a maid for doctors), but spiritually rich. I still remember when I was ten years old and my mother taught me to memorize Psalm 1, "Blessed is the man / Who walks not in the counsel of the ungodly, / . . . But his delight is in the law of the LORD, / And in His law he meditates day and night" (vv. 1a–2.). I have been reading my Bible almost every day since.

Occasionally, we would go on driving vacations to visit our many Meier relatives in Kansas, Oklahoma, Texas, and other parts of the United States. During these trips we were again reminded of those German shoe repairmen's legacy of faith and the fruit of their witness to my extended family, all of whom were devout believers.

If only those two shoe repairmen could have known how long-lasting and far-reaching their impact would be for the kingdom of Christ. What a blessing that would have been to them. They offered their profession, their hearts, and their willingness to go anywhere for God, and He multiplied their gift again and again. The decisions we make today do have lasting impact; unimaginable to us but important nonetheless. We must be mindful of this as we ask What would Jesus do? *and strive to do God's will in our professions, homes, and ministry.*

—PM

My
Short Fuse

*So then, my beloved brethren, let every man be swift to
hear, slow to speak, slow to wrath; for the wrath of man
does not produce the righteousness of God.
(James 1:19–20)*

My mother always fancied sports cars. All the while I
was growing up, she never once had the traditional
"Mom-mobile." When I got my driver's license, the
one thing I couldn't wait for was to drive her car. She had a
1976 Corvette that was absolutely beautiful. My dad had bought
it for her in 1988 from the original owner who never drove it.
The car had only twelve thousand miles on it, had never been
driven in the rain, and was still in showroom condition. It was
white with a red interior and had wide tires with chrome mags.
It was a real cherry. Mom loved her car, and I treasured it.

On occasion, Mom and Dad were nice enough to trust
me with the keys to that beautiful car. To this day, I can't
believe they let their sixteen-year-old daughter drive that car

around. Because of their trust, I always took really good care of Mom's car. I would wash and wax it on Friday afternoons so that it would be clean for the weekends. I really had fun driving my friends around and going out in that cool car.

One night I drove the 'Vette to youth group. I parked it away from everyone else's car so as not to get any door dings or scratches. After youth group was finished, all of the kids were standing around in the parking lot trying to figure out where to go to eat. As I was talking with someone, one of the kids was backing his car out of the parking lot a little too quickly, and, because it was dark, did not see my mother's Corvette. Yes, you guessed it. He backed straight into that beautiful car and ripped a big hole in the right front fender.

I was absolutely livid. This car had never been wrecked, scratched, or anything. When the kid got out of the car to see what he had done, I let him have it. Basically, I shouted out a bunch of expletives directed at the sky and then at him. What I didn't stop to realize is that this kid felt horrible for what he had done and all I could do was criticize him. In reality, I think I was attempting to humiliate him and all I did was humiliate myself.

This was a situation where I definitely did not take the time to stop and ask myself, *What would Jesus do*? My behavior was the exact opposite of how Jesus would have handled the situation. Just think of the witness I could have been if I had reacted as my parents did when I came home and showed them what happened to the car.

My parents were notably disappointed; however, they told me, "It's just a car, it can be fixed." That was it. They weren't angry, they didn't fly off the handle, nor did they blame me for "having to drive" the car to youth group. They simply said, "It's OK, it was just an accident."

I wish that is how I would have reacted. Instead, I made the poor boy who hit the car feel terrible, humiliated myself by my actions, and was further humbled when my parents were so kind about the situation. Being forgiving in such a situation would have been far more effective from a witnessing standpoint than shouting. Because of that ordeal, I have never again let my anger rise so quickly that I couldn't control what came out of my mouth.

Whenever a situation arises in which you could be easily angered or upset, simply take a deep breath and ask yourself, What would Jesus do? *I have to say, this ritual has made a big impact on how I handle various situations.*

—HG

BEFORE
ROE v. WADE

The LORD is near to those who have a broken heart,
And saves such as have a contrite spirit. (Ps. 34:18)

Thirty years ago before Wade met Roe in a courtroom and abortion was still illegal, one of my best friends found herself pregnant and unmarried. The baby's father and she really had no interest in a future together. It was his suggestion that she try to "get rid" of the baby. He said he had connections to help get her an abortion. Never mind that it was illegal.

We were twenty years old then. Until that time in our lives, abortion was not in our vocabulary and certainly not on our minds. My friend and I were both Christians though we were not seeking the Lord daily. However, we both had a heart knowledge of what God considered right and wrong and we knew He would not choose abortion.

My husband (now of twenty-nine years) and I had been dating for a year then. He was angry that I would even consider someone who was thinking of murdering her baby my friend. Those were his exact words.

Even though she and I were roommates, my friend hid her pregnancy from me for over two months, claiming the morning sickness she was having was just a bout with the flu. By the time she had the courage to tell me she was pregnant, she was almost finished with her first trimester. She told me the baby's father had given her the name of a backstreet abortionist—excuse me, "doctor." He wouldn't, however, help her pay the two hundred dollar fee so she asked me to loan her the money. I put off my answer.

She was my friend. In my heart I know I wouldn't have considered abortion for myself and yet my heart was breaking for my friend who felt this was her only answer.

Days turned into weeks and she was near her next trimester. One Sunday morning she woke me, asking me to go with her to see the doctor who had agreed to terminate her pregnancy in a little-known suburb of Dallas. It was time for me to decide what I would do.

I went with her. I gave her the money. I waited alone in a stark lobby while the doctor I never did see clanged what I hoped were sterile instruments against his metal table. I could hear her moans. I drove home without a word from her, stopping every few blocks so she could throw her guts up on the pavement. I nursed her through hemorrhaging, high fever, and anemia for a week. (The doctor asked her to avoid going to an emergency room if at all possible.) Hours after arriving back at our apartment the baby fell from her into the toilet. Some people would prefer I say fetus. Two weeks later my friend moved out. I never saw my friend again. She would not answer my letters or take my calls and so I have not spoken to her all these years. Her choice.

The Bible does promise to heal the years the locusts have eaten and in God's own way He has put something in my life that has helped heal the pain. There has been an abortion clinic in our office park since abortion became legal. These past years our company has supported an alternative clinic on our premises until that ministry moved on to another space. We have saved one hundred and twenty-five babies by directing them to our door instead of the abortion clinic next door.

The abortion clinic is still there and some days I stand looking out and pray for those going in, and some days they change their minds and leave.

What an incredible situation. When thinking about what Jesus would have done I am left with several impressions:

1. Jesus loved and ministered to sinners but was quick to point out and rebuke sin.

2. I don't believe Jesus would participate directly or indirectly in abortion. He would have continued to try and stop my friend.

3. Faced with my friend after the procedure was over, however, I'm sure Jesus would have nursed her, loved her, and forgiven her as I tried to do.

We are all faced with complex situations that may not have a clear right or wrong answer. In these instances, stand by truth and right with all your might, but do it with love, compassion, and humility.

—BC

TWO
DREAMS

*Now Joseph had a dream . . . then he dreamed still
another dream . . . (Gen. 37:5a,9a)*

Typical of many teenagers from my generation, I wanted to be just like my father when I grew up. At age sixteen, I was hoping to become a carpenter so I could work with him someday. I had no intention of going to college, let alone becoming a physician, but divine coincidences and two vivid dreams changed all that.

One Sunday at church, an elderly prayer warrior in our church, Mrs. Arnold, came up to me after service, put her hands on my shoulders and told me that she was praying daily that someday God would use me in a significant way. Though I appreciated her prayer and encouragement, I didn't spend too much time thinking about the implications of her words.

On another Sunday, a very busy surgeon who attended our church, Dr. Bob Schindler, invited me to his home that night to encourage me to memorize Proverbs 3:5–6, "Trust in the LORD with all your heart, / And lean not on your own understanding; / In all your ways acknowledge Him, / And He shall direct your paths." At home that night I did memorize those verses from Proverbs, went about my usual evening routine, went to sleep, and began dreaming.

In my first dream that night, Jesus spoke to me and told me that He wanted me to become a physician, like Dr. Schindler. So startling and vivid, the dream was incredible. I woke up stunned and certain God had just given me a direct instruction in that dream. I prayed and told God I would do what He asked and become a doctor.

After returning to sleep I had a second intense dream in which I was an older doctor, traveling around the globe as part of a team teaching things that would have an impact for Christ. Again, I awoke from the dream because of how unusually real and emotionally powerful it was. After this dream I told God I was willing to do whatever that dream meant, even if it meant becoming a foreign missionary. Less clear than the first dream, I didn't understand what the second dream meant but I did keep it in the back of my mind to reflect on from time to time.

After those two dreams, I began a college prep curriculum at school, studied harder, went on to college, graduate school, medical school, and a psychiatric specialty, finishing my schooling at age thirty. Still working on fulfilling God's vision for my life, I was blessed to spend the next decade practicing Christian psychiatry part-time while teaching future pastors and missionaries full-time at Trinity Evangelical Divinity

School in Chicago then at Dallas Theological Seminary where I finally completed my own seminary degree at age forty.

Not finished with me by a long shot, God has continued to mold me into the man I saw in my dream thirty-six years ago and now has me proclaiming His gospel and offering professional insights on a live, call-in Christian psychiatry talk show and traveling to foreign countries with a variety of different medical/psychiatric ministries. Though I couldn't have imagined it working out so perfectly at the time, because I recognized God's voice and answered His call, He has opened doors and led me in the direction He intended from the start and has blessed me beyond measure.

Thousands of years ago, the beloved seventeen-year-old son of Jacob, Joseph, dreamed two dreams that changed his life forever. Strange to him and richly symbolic, it would have been easy for Joseph to ignore these dreams and go about his business, but he didn't. Joseph recognized the dreams as communication from God, was faithful to God even in the most difficult circumstances, and in the end, was blessed beyond measure.

One of the broadest ways we can respond to the question What would Jesus do? *is to remain open to God's leading and simply listen for His*

voice. In a world filled with skeptics, humanists, and atheists, believing that God speaks in dreams, visions, and through the admonitions and wise counsel of his servants is a bold and risky proposition, but one that you must not ignore.

—PM

NEIGHBORLY
EXCITEMENT

You shall love your neighbor as yourself. (Gal. 5:14b)

In July of 1973 Norm and Becky Wretlind moved to Richardson, Texas, from California with an intense desire to share the gospel with their new neighbors. In September they held a neighborhood open house. As everyone left, Norm and Becky asked their guests to sign a little book. Each night throughout the fall, the Wretlinds would kneel with their two little daughters and pray for every name in that guest book.

As Christmas approached, Norm and Becky decided that they would hold a Christmas party for their neighbors in hopes of getting to know them on a more personal level. A special guest couple shared what Christmas meant to them as Christians and shared the gospel of Jesus Christ. That evening, a neighbor, Sharon Simonetta rededicated her life to Christ and her husband, Dennis, found Christ's forgiveness for the first time.

Norm and Becky didn't stop there. With the evangelistic excitement building in their neighborhood, they continued to share the gospel. On Valentine's Day, Becky held a coffee for the women in the neighborhood. Once again, a guest speaker came and shared the gospel. A few more neighbors came to know Christ as their Savior. There were many more women from this coffee who wanted to continue to learn more about Christ, and so, a women's neighborhood Bible study began.

Now it's time to shift this story to a more personal perspective. Dennis and Sharon Simonetta were great friends with my parents, Dwight and Hilde Johnson. During the spring after the Christmas party, Dennis, Sharon, and my parents participated in a bowling league together on Sunday nights. It was during these bowling matches that Dennis and Sharon continually shared the gospel with them and invited them to come to church numerous times. Sharon finally invited my mom to come to the weekly women's Bible study in the neighborhood.

Becky Wretlind led the studies each week and patiently answered my mom's never ending questions about God's grace. Each week as they met, my mom and Becky became closer friends. Finally, one May afternoon, Becky took my mother aside to talk with her more about salvation. It was then that my mom sat with Becky, prayed, and was born again.

Just a few days later, Dennis and Sharon had a neighborhood pool party modeled after Norm and Becky's Christmas party. They had a guest speaker, Bob George, who shared his testimony. Like my dad, Bob had lived in Germany serving in the armed forces, married a German girl, and played in a rock and roll band. My dad was truly intrigued because he had so many things in common with Bob. However, Dad realized he was missing one essential element in his life that was evident in Bob. Daddy prayed that day to receive Christ.

I am always amazed to think of how the obedience of one family to share the gospel of Christ has impacted our community throughout the last twenty-four years. God truly blessed their efforts. Hundreds of people, including me and my family, have come to know Christ because one family loved their neighbors and followed the words from Hebrews, "Remember those who rule over you, who have spoken the word of God to you, whose faith follow, considering the outcome of their conduct" (13:7). Because one family was obedient, I now have eternal life.

The seeds planted then are producing fruit to this very day. I know the Lord has continuing plans for what started in a small neighborhood in Richardson, Texas, those many years ago. My hometown church, Richland Bible Fellowship, was born out of that neighborly evangelism, and now, over three hundred families make up our church body.

Never underestimate the power of one. If you are open to the prompting of the Holy Spirit, God will accomplish much through you.

One of the hardest things Jesus wants us to do is also one of the most important—share our faith with others. Truly born out of love for our neighbors and friends, witnessing is an essential component to the life lived as Jesus would live it.
—HG

Unconditional Honor

But if any widow has children or grandchildren, let them
first learn to show piety at home and to repay their
parents; for this is good and acceptable before God.
(1 Tim. 5:4)

I am the oldest of three children my mother didn't want.
She told us that with her alcohol-slurred voice every day,
even into adulthood.

It's bittersweet irony that the older and more feeble she
became, the more comfortable she was with us. Actually, we
were her only contact with society besides television. Isolating
herself, she chose not to have any friends and had not driven
a car in more than thirty-five years. My mother seemed to look
forward to our visits and usually had a list of various household tasks she wished us to complete. After our father died,
my sister and I were always mowing the yard he had loved and
patiently tended. It had thirty-eight trees, many of which we
had helped plant. My sister and I actually looked forward to

34

each visit as an adventure—*what would happen next?* On one eventful trip home when I was almost forty, my sister and I even hot-tarred a portion of the roof.

One of the saddest memories I have of trying to help my aging mother was when I took her cat to the vet for shots. I never understood her relationship with that cat. He would hide behind her chair and then pounce around her legs. After a few seconds of this, she would kick him across the room. That describes what it was like to try to reach out to Mother. (She insisted we call her Mother—she did not want to be a "mommy.")

Anyway, back to the cat. When the cat was a kitten I placed it in a covered laundry hamper to transport it to the vet. By our next trip he had outgrown the hamper so I put him in a cardboard box and closed the top over him. He was not happy. I now know how they came up with the image of Garfield suction-cupped to a car window—they put him in a box first!

Well, trying to escape the cat's wrath after he freed himself from the box, I made the mistake of opening the car door. In a flash my mother's house cat escaped into the hill country of Texas. I expected my easily angered mother to be livid; instead, she did her best to ease my own misery. She said, "It's all right. Thank you for trying. You did your best." I knew she wanted to cry with every word.

At age sixty-five she developed Alzheimer's symptoms. After extensive tests her doctor said she had a mix of Parkinson's disease and brain cell loss resulting from years of alcohol abuse. Bless her heart, though, after fifty-five years of smoking, emphysema is what finally ended her life.

Three years before her death she became incontinent and lost her ability to speak. Because she needed twenty-four-hour care, I moved her to a nursing home a few minutes from my home.

Some weeks I was there every day to feed her lunch and dinner. She wouldn't take her eyes from my face during these visits. I know she knew what was going on around her even though she couldn't respond.

Eventually she didn't have the strength to go to the dining room so my visits were confined to her room, organizing her few personal belongings, adjusting the television and doing her hair and nails while keeping up a chatty dialogue with her roommates. These three precious ladies went home to the Lord before my mother did.

I know my mother is with the Lord because during her confinement to "God's waiting room," my brother-in-law led her to the Lord before she lost her ability to nod her head. The few months after that we took communion together and that first Christmas, my mother, who had never stepped foot inside a church, miraculously sang at the residents' dining room Christmas service. Still more amazing is that she knew every word to each Christmas carol sung.

My last visit with her was on my forty-seventh birthday. I decided to spend the day with her. The last time I had been with my mother on my birthday was the day I turned seventeen, two days before I had moved away from home.

This day she appeared so frail, all seventy-seven pounds of her. The residents' beautician had just given her a perm so I didn't have much to do. Watching me move around the room, she would look at the family photos on the wall and then back at me. All the time I had the feeling she wanted to say something. I quizzed her, but she would only keep moving her eyes from the pictures to my face. The look she had reminded me of the day I lost her cat and, even though the word *love* was never spoken in our house, the words she gave me with her eyes were words that I felt were in her heart. She couldn't speak but there was a tear or two in her eyes and at that moment I felt she was affirming our relationship, "It's all right. Thank you for trying. You did your best."

Relationships don't come with guarantees of returned love or even of returned kindness. Yet, Paul instructs us in his letter to "show piety at home," and Jesus again and again commands us to love — neighbors, parents, children. Filled with dysfunctional families, society often encourages adult children of abusive parents to simply walk away from mothers and fathers,

leaving them behind forever. This is not God's way. Showing piety at home does not mean tolerating abuse; however, it does mean loving even in desperate circumstances.

—BC

INCURABLE

Confess your trespasses to one another, and pray for one another, that you may be healed. (James 5:16a)

In June of 1993 I received a phone call from Sweden. A Lutheran minister had read one of my books. He told me about his five children and his wife who he loved dearly. Unfortunately, his wife had some psychological difficulties and was considered incurable by her psychiatrists. In fact, she had just been committed for life to a Swedish mental hospital. This beleaguered man said he had very little money but needed my advice. *What would Jesus do?*

I told this man to bring his wife to Dallas where my team and I would treat her for free at our Paul Meier New Life Day Hospital for eight hours a day until she got well. This woman had severe depression, frequent full-blown panic attacks, severe insomnia, headaches, allergies, and phobias. Though more complicated than most, her disorders were nongenetic and not too different from thousands of others we have treated at our clinics throughout America using biblical, insight-oriented therapy. She seemed fairly typical to our team.

We ask our patients about all the significant people in their lives, studying our patients' body language to discover the root causes of their symptoms. When we asked Joyce, the pastor's wife, about her children or her husband, she seemed at peace; but whenever we mentioned her mother or father, she had an autonomic nervous system response. Dilated pupils, tears in her eyes, red blotches on her neck, as well as other telltale signs assured us that her cure would come by exposing Joyce to the truth about her bitterness toward her parents. This, in turn, would enable her to truly forgive them and also to forgive herself for the false guilt and shame that always come when a young girl or boy is abused by parents.

Sure enough, her parents both physically and sexually abused her repeatedly throughout her life. When we found out they had never even given her a birthday party, we threw a party for her, even though it wasn't her birthday, and bought her a teddy bear. We used Gestalt techniques to get her in touch with her true emotions of rage and bitterness. One time we put two empty chairs in front of her and persuaded her to pretend her mom and dad were sitting in the chairs. We had her call each of them by name and tell them how she felt, then, with the help of almighty God, forgive them. We encouraged her, though, to never see her parents again because they continued to be verbally abusive toward her.

Within three weeks, she was totally cured, happy, at peace

with herself and with God, and went back to her psychiatrists in Sweden. They were so amazed that they wrote articles about Joyce's "miracle cure" in America in several major newspapers throughout Sweden.

A year later, Joyce and her husband, Dan, called me from Sweden again. This time they asked me, "If we send letters to all five thousand psychiatrists and psychologists in Sweden and have a one week conference on Christian psychiatry, will you come and teach it?" So in June of 1994, I went to Sweden.

Dan and Joyce charged three hundred dollars each for the seminar, and one hundred mental health professionals came. Many of them were already believers and others became believers during that week of training. Dan and Joyce shared the story of her childhood and her cure, and many of them wept. By the end of the week, fifty of these professionals made a firm commitment to have Christian clinics that integrated Scripture as their firm foundation in their counseling.

Dan and Joyce paid for my airfare and took the thirty thousand dollars they raised from the seminar and left the pastorate to head up the whole Christian psychology movement in Sweden. One female psychiatrist joined them and donates half of her earnings to support the ongoing movement. Together, they meet with the new Christian clinics around Sweden, teaching scriptural principles and passing around the tapes of my seminar.

It was a clear and easy decision for me to offer to help Joyce with the resources at my disposal. Of course this is what Jesus would have me do. What may not be so obvious, is the way that Dan and Joyce did what Jesus would have them do. First, Dan was incredibly brave and had much trust in God's healing power to step out in faith and call me from Sweden. He knew God could heal his wife and pursued every opportunity he could think of to work toward that end.

Second, Joyce showed amazing grace and generosity by sharing her devastating family history and then her spectacular recovery with thousands of Christians and mental health professionals. She is a walking testament to the astounding power of Christ's love and forgiveness. These two lovely people are a shining example of stepping out in faith and doing Jesus' will.

—PM

THE LITTLE
DRUMMER BOY

Therefore, as the elect of God, holy and beloved, put on
tender mercies, kindness, humility, meekness,
longsuffering. (Col. 3:12)

It was the spring of 1956 in Glenfield, North Dakota. Like most rural towns in middle America, Glenfield was a very small farming community. Children attending school in Glenfield came from all over the county and other surrounding areas.

Alton Hegvik directed the band at Glenfield High School. Well-known throughout the state, Mr. Hegvik was one of the best. His marching band always won top honors at competitions and participated in parades from time to time.

At the end of March, it was once again time for Mr. Hegvik to organize his marching band for the upcoming Memorial Day parade in nearby Jamestown. Because Glenfield High was so small, Mr. Hegvik had to compile his band from children in the seventh through twelfth grades.

In addition to his duties with the high school and junior high, Mr. Hegvik also instructed a band class for the elementary students. There was one student in his elementary school class to whom Mr. Hegvik paid special attention. Little Dwight Johnson was eleven years old and in the fifth grade. An average clarinet player for his age, Dwight's musical abilities weren't really anything to brag about. Mr. Hegvik knew that Dwight was having a difficult time at home. Dwight's mother, Angie, had been sick for nearly two years and was dying of cancer. Homebound for more than a year, Angie spent most of her time in bed. Unfortunately, in 1956 there was not much that could be done to save her. There weren't many bright moments for Dwight and his parents during that time. It was very difficult for Dwight and his dad to know that they would soon lose the woman they both so dearly loved.

Mr. Hegvik was a friend of the family and knew how much music meant to Dwight's mother. Angie just loved it and always listened to records or the radio. Music was her only entertainment. This was partly why Dwight played the clarinet and also took piano lessons. His mother so enjoyed listening to him play.

Knowing all of this, Mr. Hegvik decided to make an unusual addition to his marching band. One day at school, Mr. Hegvik asked Dwight to play a big part in the marching band. He knew Dwight was not good enough to play the clarinet with the band, so he told him that he could play the big bass drum. Dwight was so excited for the opportunity. It was a really big deal to be a part of the marching band, especially for a fifth grader. This would be the first time anyone from elementary school had been asked to march with the high school band.

Mr. Hegvik brought Dwight to the band hall and outfitted him with a brand new uniform and a bass drum. Dwight could hardly wait to get home to tell his mother and show her his new uniform and the big drum he was going to play.

He arrived home that afternoon, put on his new uniform, started beating his new drum, and came into his mother's room. For the first time in quite awhile, Angie was beaming with excitement. She was so proud that her son would be marching with the band on Memorial Day.

Memorial Day came, and it was time for the Johnsons to head for Jamestown to march with the band. Though usually too sick to get out of bed, Angie was determined that on this day she would go and see her son play with the Glenfield marching band. It was the nicest day she had spent with her husband and son in almost two years.

Two weeks later, Angie's battle with cancer ended and she passed away. I'm sorry that I never got to meet my grandmother. I know she was a wonderful lady and I know our shared love for music would have drawn us close together. Nonetheless, I'm thankful to Mr. Hegvik for his kindness and compassion toward my father and his mother. By demonstrating Christlike compassion, Mr. Hegvik enabled my father and his family to enjoy one more great memory before his mother died.

I don't think we ever fully realize the impact our compassion can have on others. I'm sure Mr. Hegvik never knew how much letting my father march with the band meant to my father and his mother. Through his actions, Mr. Hegvik displayed those characteristics of kindness and compassion that were exemplified in Jesus each and every day that He walked this earth. Whether he actually asked himself the question or not when he asked my dad to march, Mr. Hegvik lived out WWJD? in that gift he gave to my family so many years ago.

—HG

A Lesson
Before Dying

And he arose and came to his father. But when he was
still a great way off, his father saw him and had
compassion, and ran and fell on his neck and kissed him.
(Luke 15:20)

My brother has been in prison three times. All of his offenses were committed trying to support his heroin habit that began at age seventeen during a tour with the marines. Forty-three years old now, my brother has been clean and sober for some time and is doing well on his own.

At the time of his first conviction, my brother was almost twenty-one. Sentenced to eleven years for felony forgery, he had stolen social security checks from my father's best friend's mailbox, forged his signature, and cashed the checks.

Six years before this incident, our father had a massive heart attack and began a roller-coaster ride of health with many dips we thought would lead to his death. He fought a good fight against his heart disease for seventeen years.

During my brother's first incarceration, he and my father spoke on the phone a few times, and early in my brother's stay my mother, father, and sister were able to visit him for a short time. Toward the end of my father's life, he wanted to see his son one last time and assure him that he loved him, had always loved him, and nothing my brother could do would change that.

One of my dad's favorite pastimes was to go for a ride with his dog, Rebel, in his classic Ford Ranchero pickup. Though old, ill-equipped, and worn out, that truck was like a Rolls Royce to my dad.

Early one Saturday morning, my father told my mother he had to see their son. He planned to drive his battered truck from central Texas to northeast Texas to the facility from which he last received a letter from my brother. He said good-bye to my mother and headed north for a seven-hour drive alone with only his thoughts and passing cars for company. (Rebel stayed home for this trip.)

Reaching his destination, my father was informed at the gate that my brother wasn't at this prison; he had been moved to the southeast Texas facility. He called my mother, told her he was heading to Huntsville for yet another seven-hour drive. My mother then called me to tell me what was going on.

Aware of both my father's ailing health and his stubborn determination, I lost it. I burst into tears, locked myself in my bathroom, and stayed there until we heard from my dad again. Seven hours later my father stood at another gate and was informed that my brother had been moved to yet another facility an hour and a half away. Of course, my dad would go. I was inconsolable. I just knew this trip was going to kill him. Every time the phone rang, I thought it was the highway patrol.

After more than sixteen hours on the road, my dad arrived at the last gate. Again, my brother wasn't there. Even if he had been there it turns out my dad had come on the wrong day to visit! Later we found out my brother had been on a medical transit. Ironic, huh?

Twenty-four hours and fifteen hundred miles later, my exhausted dad arrived home. I talked to him for the first time since his decision to make this futile trip. He assured me he was all right, but beyond that, he said nothing.

I recently learned that my father wrote a letter to my brother telling him what he was going to say that day. I don't know the contents of the letter, and I don't know if it still exists. My dad died shortly after that trip having never seen his son again. My brother was not able to attend the funeral. Daddy was buried in a military cemetery with a solemn three-gun salute. The flag draped over his casket was a fitting tribute. When the flag was carefully removed, folded, and the lone casket exposed, I thought about this man, alone and vulnerable all his life because he sacrificed so much for others. I regret not telling him enough how much I appreciated what he did for our family and wanted to do for me.

The lesson, though obvious, is one that is frequently missed. My dad's effort to make amends with my brother took an extraordinary physical and emotional toll on him but he never even thought to count the cost. We shouldn't either.

—BC

THE
GOLDEN RULE

Therefore, whatever you want men to do to you, do also to them, for this is the Law and the Prophets. (Matt. 7:12)

Growing up in Saginaw, Michigan, I was the third of four children. I dearly love my brother and both of my sisters. As circumstances had it, I spent more time with my little sister Nancy than either of my other siblings because she was the only one I could boss around, given that she was four years younger than me. But by the time I left elementary school, Nancy and I were best friends with no more fights.

Now, Nancy Meier is Nancy Brown and runs one of our affiliated New Life Clinics in Wheaton, Illinois. Her four sons (my nephews) all attended Wheaton College in that same town. Her oldest son, Jeff Brown, was an all-American quarterback for Wheaton's football team in 1996. In the fall of 1997 her other three sons started for the Wheaton College soccer team.

In November of 1997 Nancy called me with a special request. Wheaton's soccer team had gone undefeated, had won its first few playoff games, and was headed for the final four to try and win the Division III national championship in Fredericksburg, Virginia. Nancy wanted to know if my wife, Jan, and I could come to watch the Brown boys play soccer and get in some quality time as couples with her and her husband, Dave.

I'm quite ashamed to admit that I told Nancy no. I said that if the game were closer to Dallas, I would happily drive there and see it. But since it was so far away, I couldn't possibly go because I would miss seeing my day hospital patients and miss a few days of my live call-in talk show. In the back of my mind I was also thinking about the expense of two airline tickets, rental car, hotel, and meals—and reminding myself that several of our children are still in college, eating up our diminishing funds!

Nancy was very sweet and accepted my answer without laying a guilt trip on me. God wasn't quite so nice! Later that night He laid quite a big guilt trip on me when I asked Him, *What would Jesus do?*

After a little prayer together, my wife and I decided to take the time and spend the money to go to the soccer final four. Another psychiatrist covered for me at the hospital, and my friends, Steve Arterburn, John Townsend, and Henry Cloud did just fine without me on the radio.

Well, Wheaton won their first game and then played the

previous year's national champion in the final game. The whole team—the Crusaders—played with great heart and with great Christian ethics as well. All three of Nancy Brown's boys starred in the game, with Eric (Scott and Skip's younger brother) scoring all three goals as Wheaton won 3–0. We all cried together afterwards and shared a memory we will talk about one thousand years from now in heaven. Of course my sister would have understood had we not made it to that special event. But had my children been in similar circumstances, you bet I'd want Nancy there to share in our family's joy! Thank goodness Jesus prompted my wife and me to reconsider *WWJD?* and to remember the golden rule.

Little kindnesses and actions are often the first to suffer at the hands of a busy life. But these acts of friendship, politeness, and togetherness are what make the world wonderful. Jesus brings home the point in the best way possible by asking us to think about how we want to be treated and then treat others that way ourselves.

—PM

THE IRONY OF
LIFE AND DEATH

You shall not murder. (Ex. 20:13)

Yes, it's God's law. It's even number six on His top ten list. To this day I am shocked at how many individuals take this so lightly. Even if a person is not a Christian, surely there should be some innate feeling or common respect for the sanctity of life.

One afternoon back in college, I was over at my boyfriend's apartment. There were always a lot of people coming and going from there. That afternoon in particular, a girl from one of my classes came over with her boyfriend. She and I decided to walk over to Braum's and get some ice cream and chat for a while. We started talking about school and some of the problems we were having with one of our professors. She also explained to me why she had missed several classes over the past few weeks. She told me that she had had an abortion.

At first, I found myself sitting there stunned. I didn't know

54

what to say. Part of my shock was that she would choose me to confide in. We weren't really friends, just classmates.

What would Jesus do? Despite my beliefs as a Christian, I knew it wouldn't be right for me to rant and rave about how wrong abortion was. Jesus didn't yell at sinners. He gently spoke to them about God's grace and forgiveness. Whenever we forcibly project our opinions on someone else, we come across as judgmental. That was the one thing I definitely did not want to do. It wasn't my right to do so. I did feel it was necessary to tell her about God's provision for life and its sanctity. Deep down, I think she knew what she did wasn't right. It wasn't my place to sit there and rub it in. I tried to console her a little; however, I did tell her that one day she would probably regret her decision. She agreed.

I know you've probably heard most of the stories. Thousands of women have abortions every day. Some do it for medical reasons, others simply use it as a form of birth control. I've heard all the excuses, "It's just tissue," "It doesn't hurt the fetus," or "If it wasn't for me the fetus wouldn't survive on its own anyway." Three days after conception that fetus has a heartbeat and it starts to develop brain waves (thought patterns). Its life begins at the moment of conception.

I once got into a heated discussion with a young man who used the excuse, "The fetus couldn't survive without the mother anyway; it's just tissue." I ventured to say, "I stand here before you made of cells, bone, blood, and tissue, no different than a fetus. I'm just a little more developed. I can guarantee you that if you left a three-year-old in the wilderness alone, that child would not survive. So what's the difference?"

Just a few weeks ago, some friends of my family had a miscarriage at five months. They found out that the baby had a severe defect, and within a matter of days she had a stillbirth. I grieved for them, but I know I couldn't fully understand their burden because I had not been through it myself. I suppose this circumstance of loss is where I find one of life's most tragic ironies. How is it that one expectant mother can casually go to a clinic to have a healthy fetus destroyed, while another's heart bleeds with sorrow for the loss of her child. It makes the mindset of the former seem all the more cruel.

Each child is a miracle from the Lord. The gift of life is just that, a gift. I have three nephews under the age of three. Sometimes I find myself just staring at them amazed. Watching them learn to crawl, to eat with a spoon, or to sound out new words is such a joy. Each child is very special and unique. Their innocence in exploration and learning is something we can all draw upon.

The abortion issue seems to have been swept under the rug somewhat by our society. Every decade seems to have its moral issue and the decade of abortion appears to be fading. My prayer is that as Christians we will not forget to do as Jesus would, and strive to protect the sanctity of life. Not to judge others for their actions, but to offer a freedom for all through Christ's grace and forgiveness.

For You formed my inward parts;
You covered me in my mother's womb.
I will praise You, for I am fearfully and
*   wonderfully made;*
Marvelous are Your works,
And that my soul knows very well.
My frame was not hidden from You,
When I was made in secret,
And skillfully wrought in the lowest parts of the
*   earth.*
Your eyes saw my substance, being yet
*   unformed.*
And in Your book they all were written,
The days fashioned for me,
When as yet there were none of them.
(Ps. 139:13–16)

—HG

GRAND THEFT TIME

*But they all with one accord began to make excuses. The
first said to him, "I have bought a piece of ground, and I
must go and see it. I ask you to have me excused."*
(Luke 14:18)

There are many ways we all cheat and thieve. Too harsh, you say? You don't have to sit at a school desk to cheat, or steal something with a price tag to be a thief. We're fortunate we don't get prosecuted for stealing time—not time we have wasted, but rather excuses we have made to get out of doing something we should. Have you ever lied or stretched the truth a little to get off from work? I have.

I have been on my own since I was seventeen. My dad paid my tuition to a merchandising college, but I had to support myself in every other area of my life. I was fortunate to land a job at a fashionable department store and rise from gift wrapping to assistant buyer for women's sportswear before I was twenty years old.

My supervisor, the head buyer, was a very nice person. But like most young upstarts, I totally discounted that this kind woman might have a life outside our narrow department of clothing racks, open-to-buy, and end-of-the-month sales. I assumed she couldn't possibly understand my needs when I wanted to have a weekend off to join my friends at a lake party. First mistake.

Rather than run the risk of my boss rejecting my request for time off, I decided to use my dad's heart disease as an excuse to take off work that weekend. Second mistake. I told my boss that my dad was having another bad spell and asked her for a few days off to go visit him. I rationalized to myself that he was, in fact, sick, even though I wasn't really going to see him this time. Another mistake.

My boss was full of compassion and concern though this didn't exactly register with me at the time. It never occurred to me that she might want to do something for my family. Biggest mistake! She went to one of my friends who was also working at the store to find out my parents' address so she could send flowers.

Well, my girlfriend (who knew my real weekend plans) did the noble thing. She told my boss what I was actually doing. I know my boss felt betrayed and humiliated.

The night before I went back to work my friend warned me that my boss knew I had deceived her. I paid a dear price for that deception. I lost my boss's trust, respect, and what I now know was a dear friendship with a valued mentor. From that day forward my boss rarely made eye contact with me and seldom discussed the day-to-day happenings of our department. She had waited a few days before confronting me with my deed. Waiting for the ax to fall was horrid! The confrontation was worse. My boss was very pleasant in her delivery of her disappointment in me and how betrayed she felt. She said that she hoped I had a good weekend at her and the store's expense. Her words convicted and pierced my soul, as they should have.

Shortly after that, my life took a turn, and I left to get married. I'll never know whether I might have jeopardized further advances in my career by that senseless act.

My husband and I have had our own business these past twenty-nine years and we have hired many people. Most of our employees have been valued, conscientious workers. Some employees have stolen time from us with excuses, laziness, or deliberate stolen hours on time cards. I cannot condone it but I can't cast the first stone either.

Who did what Jesus would? Clearly, not me. My boss, when under the impression that my father was ill, showed compassion and generosity as an employer and as a friend. And when confronted with my dishonesty, she didn't lash out in anger or fire me (though justified). She rightly expressed her disappointment and then moved

on. *The contrast between her behavior and mine is stark.*

The second lesson here is that being honest and truthful, in little things as well as big, is the ideal Jesus deserves from all of us.

—BC

My
Bloody Hands

*When I say to the wicked, "O wicked man, you shall
surely die!" and you do not speak to warn the wicked from
his way, that wicked man shall die in his iniquity; but his
blood I will require at your hand. (Ezek. 33:8)*

I trusted Christ as my Savior at the age of six because of the
encouragement of a very loving Sunday school teacher,
Mrs. Brooks. At age sixteen, I dedicated my life to Christ
very privately, in my own bedroom, after having two significant, God-given dreams. A few years later, at age eighteen and
a freshman in college, God was ready to teach me another
WWJD? lesson.

Since age ten, when my mom helped me memorize Psalm
1, especially verse two ("But his delight is in the law of the
LORD, / And in His law he meditates day and night."), I have
been reading my Bible every day. So, when in college, I arose
every morning and read my Bible before doing anything else.
It was 1963, and the Vietnam War was heating up.

One morning my reading was in Ezekiel 33. After reading the first three verses I had to stop because my nose started bleeding for no apparent reason. I caught the dripping blood on my hands and quickly leaned my head back until it stopped. I decided to keep on reading the chapter with blood-smeared hands before cleaning up.

Then I came to verse eight. I began weeping because God showed me that I was doing very little witnessing to nonbelievers, and they were dying and going to hell. It was their blood on my hands. On my knees I promised God I would look for occasions to witness to people about salvation in Christ. Later that day I heard about an opportunity to go every Saturday to a Christian servicemen's center to speak with young soldiers preparing to be shipped off to Vietnam. I asked myself WWJD? and did it. But I was quite shy back then and scared to death to talk to strangers in uniform, especially about Jesus.

That first Saturday I prayed intensely that God would make the first soldier easy to talk to, to build my confidence. I told God that I thought I could handle future rejections if at least the first witnessing experience didn't go too badly.

As I was standing on the street in front of the center, silently praying that intense prayer, a soldier walked up behind me and tapped me on the shoulder. I was startled, but turned around to ask him what he wanted. To my total shock, he asked me if I was a Christian. I told him that I was, and he told me he had an unusual request. Then he told me that he had received a letter from his mother the previous night. In the letter, his mother expressed fear that her son might end up dying in Vietnam, and she asked him to trust in Christ so he could go to heaven if he died. Then the soldier asked me if I could show him how to become a Christian.

I took this young soldier into the center and showed him the promises of salvation found in Romans 3:23, Romans 6:23, John 1:12, and John 3:16. I was blessed to be able to lead that soldier and three hundred other soldiers to Christ that year on my Saturdays. I look forward to meeting them again someday in heaven, where some of them are already.

It is imperative that we share the salvation message with nonbelievers. This is one of the great requests Jesus makes of us. But the wonderful thing about following Jesus' will is that He will give us the confidence and strength necessary to carry out His requests. All we have to do is ask What would Jesus do?

—PM

SHINING
LIGHT

Let your light so shine before men, that they may see your
good works and glorify your Father in heaven.
(Matt. 5:16)

As I look back on my life, I can see what a difference the
question *What would Jesus do?* has made in my life.
Before this past year, I had never heard the popularly
coined phrase *WWJD?*. However, the thought and practice
was instilled in me from childhood.

I had the fortune of growing up in a household in which
I was strictly disciplined—not excessively, just consistently.
My mother always backed up her discipline with Scripture,
showing me why what I did was not right. She used the characteristics of Christ to teach me right from wrong, to love and
respect others, to share, to give, and the list goes on.

In a world where good examples are hard to find, it is
increasingly important for Christians to take a stand so that
we might establish a standard of biblical morals and ethics.

Christlike morals and ethics are what build good character and strong relationships with others. Our society today is divided about what aspects of a person's character are the basis for a good code of morals and ethics. Society fumbles around in a state of confusion because it has no model to follow, but we do.

As a Christian, you will be challenged every day by different individuals and situations that will either bring out the best or worst in you. How you react to each situation places your reputation as a Christian on the line. It's a reputation that we, as followers of Christ, can't afford to sacrifice.

Jesus Christ is our foundation. He not only came and died for our sakes, but He lived life on earth to give us the perfect picture of righteousness. In Matthew 5:48 Christ tells us, "Therefore you shall be perfect, just as your Father in heaven is perfect." He challenges us to strive for that perfect righteousness. At times it can be demoralizing. I can't think of anything more difficult than trying to live up to the standards of Christ, but that's where the incredible depth of the grace of Christ can be experienced.

The Father knew long ago that we couldn't attain perfection on our own. That's why, in His mercy, He sent His Son to die in our place. If you have never trusted in Jesus Christ as your personal Savior, may I invite you to experience a depth of grace and forgiveness like never before. He is waiting for you with open arms. Just claim in your heart John 3:16, "For God so loved the world that He gave His only begotten

Son, that whoever believes in Him should not perish but have everlasting life."

Whether a lifelong Christian or a brand new believer, we all strive to walk with Jesus and let our light shine for Him. Asking oneself the question WWJD? is just the beginning to a full life in Christ. To support this discipline we must regularly read God's Word, fellowship with other believers, and allow Christ to do His perfect will through us. May you endure in His love, find peace in His rest, and remember to walk with Jesus daily.

—HG

HOMELESS – PLEASE HELP!

So let each one give as he purposes in his heart, not grudgingly or of necessity; for God loves a cheerful giver. (2 Cor. 9:7)

So much controversy surrounds street-corner beggars. Some cities have made it unlawful to loiter and ask for handouts, while other cities regulate the hours the homeless can be visible to the public. Some of the most outspoken comments I've heard on this subject come from Christians. Have you ever heard, "He's not really homeless" or "He would rather beg than work for food" or "I never give them anything" or how about "They're a nuisance hanging on every corner like 'they' do."

I frequently pass street corners where some people are regulars. I don't know their circumstances and certainly cannot judge their motives for asking for handouts, but I do want to help those truly in need. In my attempts to help, I know I've been suckered by some real experts. I guess that's the price I'll pay in order to help even one genuinely distressed person.

In Luke 14:13 and 14 Jesus tells us to invite those who cannot repay us to our dinners. I would like to think I would. Wouldn't you?

I can't pull up beside women, children, or amputees without giving them something. One month, a particular mother and daughter were at the same traffic corner almost every day. It seemed I was always at the front of the turning lane beside them. One of the many times my window came down to give them my change, the little girl spoke. It was freezing outside and she said , "I like your car." I said, "Thank you." (I wanted to let her in but her mother was wary.) I asked her mother if they were all right. She told me they were trying to get enough money to move on to someplace warmer. "Alabama," she said. The light changed and before I could circle my car around and get back to where they were to see how I could further help, they were gone. I never saw them again, but I still wonder if they made it.

On another occasion, my husband and I were driving from Texas to Colorado and made our usual fast food stop. As my husband got out of the car, a dirty vagrant came up to him and asked him to give him enough money to eat dinner. My husband said, "I would rather you come inside the restaurant and let me buy you whatever you want in there." The man hesitated but eventually went along.

My husband later told me that the line in the restaurant

literally parted from the man's stench, and even though he was with my husband, the people at the counter didn't want to wait on him. You would have to know my husband to visualize the look he exchanged across the counter as he said, "Give him anything he wants." The workers were indignant, but both men left with their bag of burgers. As he left, the man shook my husband's hand saying, "Thanks, man." Whatever his circumstances, this man's dignity was left intact because of my husband's help.

When confronted with people in need, Jesus wants us to "purpose" in our own hearts what we want to do for people less fortunate than ourselves. If we do this, then we won't have to think whether or not the receiver "deserves" it the next time someone asks for our assistance. God knows their hearts, and God knows ours.

—BC

Tongue-Stabbing

And the tongue is a fire, a world of iniquity.
(James 3:6a)

When I was six years old and proudly entering the first grade in a public elementary school, I was new in the neighborhood. I didn't really know any of the other kids and was a little shy, but I still wanted to be everyone's favorite. I used every skill I knew of at that young age to gain favor with the other kids.

I was always the first kid done when we had quizzes and felt the scorn of my peers for finishing first, so I quickly learned that acting a little dumb actually made me more popular. I would wait until a few other kids turned in their papers before I would turn mine in so I wouldn't look too nerdy. I practiced sports with my big brother so I would be picked a little sooner during recess games. I learned that if you hit little girls on the back of the head with a book (but not hard), it was a form of flirting and the girls would actually like you more and the boys would laugh. And I learned that if you compliment your friends, they would like you in direct proportion to how important you made them feel.

Now, none of these skills were too bad for an awkward six-year-old son of German immigrant parents living in a lower middle class neighborhood. But I also learned one horrible skill. It's called tongue-stabbing. Basically, it's putting down selected peers so you can look better to the rest of your peers. Unfortunately, it works quite well. Even in my own Christian family, where I was the third of four children, I learned to act "righteous" around my parents, never letting them see the bad parts of my attitudes and behaviors, thereby gaining points with them. My mother is still alive and well at ninety and still thinks I was sinless. (Just ask her.)

I remember one boy in my first grade class who suffered under my tongue-stabbing. He was actually a very nice boy; let's call him Ronnie Mueller. Ronnie had some sort of allergic condition, so he always had a congested nose. I was jealous of him because he was better than me at hitting the softball at recess. So I began making fun of him and telling the other kids that Ronnie had "cooties" because of his snotty nose. To my delight, they all joined in and wouldn't even touch the stairway banister if Ronnie touched it because they might catch his cooties.

Still a little careless in covering up my crimes, I made a major tactical error. I forgot to deliver a note I had written about Ronnie's cooties and my mom found it in my pants when I changed clothes later that day. She then showed it to my dad, who explained to me how cruel this was. Then, to be sure I remembered his lesson, my dad got out the family paddle and gave me a spanking I still remember today, more from my guilt than from the intensity of the swing. It was the most important spanking I ever got, and I honestly thank God for it now.

When I went into full-time Christian work at age thirty I read a book by a great preacher from the past—Harry Ironside. He said that if you devote your life to serving Christ with all your heart, you will get a little criticism from the world and a lot of criticism from your fellow Christians who are jealous of you. Tongue-stabbing! He said the Christian army is the only army in the world that goes around stabbing its own wounded soldiers. I couldn't believe that when I was thirty, but within a few years I found it to be quite true.

As a Christian psychiatrist, I have had Christian leaders write nasty magazine articles and even books about me and other Christian psychiatrists and psychologists. I call them up and try to tell them what they say about me is not at all true, but the truth is irrelevant to them. They turn around and say lies about me even right after I tell them what I really believe. But I ask myself *WWJD?* and remember my dad's spanking. I do indeed understand the damaging power of tongue stabbing and pray that Jesus will always allow my tongue to be used for healing, not wounding.

What is said by the tongue is often a reflection of what is in the heart. In order to tame your tongue you may need to soften your heart. If you find yourself engaging in tongue-stabbing ask WWJD?, *apologize, and encourage humility and love in your heart, which is the true fruit of a life lived for Christ.*

—*PM*

Two Blessings in Disguise

For You formed my inward parts;
You covered me in my mother's womb.
I will praise You, for I am fearfully and
  wonderfully made;
Marvelous are Your works,
And that my soul knows very well. (Ps. 139:13–14)

My one and only brother is seven years older than I am. When I was little he teased me constantly, probably because I pestered him so much. Even though we didn't get along at times, he always looked out for me when the neighborhood bully was around, played with me even when he didn't want to, and gave me lots of big brother love. Through the years we have become great friends.

Dwight married in the spring of 1991 when I was a senior in high school. He and his wife, Vicki, had both graduated from Baylor University where he was pursuing a career as a pilot. Eventually, Dwight joined the army as a warrant officer in order to fly helicopters.

Dwight and Vicki moved to Fort Rucker, Alabama, for flight school and started a family there. My first nephew, Dylan, was born while Dwight was at Fort Rucker. A year after Dylan's arrival, Dwight finished flight school and the army shipped him off for what turned out to be a two-year tour in South Korea. Vicki and Dylan were not able to visit him for the first five months of his tour.

That August, Vicki and Dylan headed off to be with Dwight for three months (the maximum visit permitted by the army). This began a series of three-month visitations, with Vicki and Dylan traveling back and forth from the states to South Korea. The only time Dwight was able to come home was for a few weeks at Christmas.

Needless to say, this was a difficult time for our family as we were separated by the Pacific Ocean. However, we were so glad Vicki and Dylan were able to spend time with Dwight. When Dylan was about twenty months old, Dwight and Vicki surprised us with the wonderful news that Vicki was pregnant again.

The first few months of Vicki's pregnancy were pretty bad. Constantly sick with nausea and even some food poisoning, Vicki endured all of this while in South Korea.

Four months into her pregnancy, Vicki went to the military hospital to have some routine tests done on the fetus. The tests came back positive for spina bifida. Babies with this condition are slightly or severely deformed and have some mental challenges. Dwight and Vicki were naturally devastated at the news. I still remember the night my brother called from South Korea, weeping and sick with worry. You can imagine how we felt for them and the baby, unable to provide physical support and comfort.

Through their tears, Dwight and Vicki remained strong. Faced with similar circumstances, many couples in our society today would choose to abort. Not Dwight and Vicki. Jesus teaches us about the sanctity of all life; so there was only one option for my brother and his wife. *What would Jesus do?* Dwight answered that question when he declared how they would love their baby no matter what, maybe even love it more.

Since there was no equipment on Dwight's remote military base for a sonogram, Vicki left for Seoul, South Korea, three days later to see a doctor for a complete exam of the baby. My mother, father, and I got down on our knees each day and prayed for Dwight, Vicki, and this new precious life. God had granted us peace about it, and we knew we would join together to love and care for that baby no matter what. After days of laying our burdens at the foot of the cross, God answered our prayers.

The phone call was magnificent. Not only was the baby fine, but there were two of them. We sobbed with overwhelming joy. What tremendous blessings God gave the Johnson family. Barrett James and Brandon Jack were born on July 10, 1996, weighing in at just over seven pounds each.

In Christ's deepest despair He turned to the Father for comfort. By laying down our burdens, not only did we receive a great deal of peace and comfort, but God also miraculously answered our prayers.

—HG

MIRROR, MIRROR
ON THE WALL

"Vanity of vanities," says the Preacher; "Vanity of vanities,
all is vanity." (Eccl. 1:2)

Just recently, I heard that many baby boomers can expect to live between one hundred and one hundred twenty years. Did you know there is a boomer institute for such studies? The newsmagazine host said, "Why would I want to do that? I'm already tired." I feel sorry for her. This theory of longevity creates a new dilemma among my peers and myself. If we are going to live that long, what are we going to look like?

Some of my friends have had face lifts and the results are incredible. It makes cosmetic junkies like me very jealous. I never leave the house without first applying my creatively planned and time consuming "mask." Bold captions on magazine covers like, "Quick Techniques for De-aging," jump out at me in checkout lines. Or how about "Lose Ten Pounds this Weekend?" I find myself listening for new wonder products and affordable techniques that will help me recapture a youthful appearance, maybe even look *better* than I thought I looked when I was in my twenties. Imagine! Several years ago a couple of us boomers, then still thirty-somethings, recognized the absurdity of our "battle" against aging.

One Friday night, the women in our church had a lock-in slumber party. The plan for the evening was to play games, eat, fellowship, stay up all night, or bring a bedroll to sleep on in any of the rooms in the learning center. We rented a large-screen television and classic movies. We had great fun that night, and toward the wee hours of the morning, some of us became party poopers and decided we needed sleep.

Now the twenty-somethings just plopped their pillows down, closed their eyes, and were fast asleep in minutes. The thirty-somethings had their nightly regimens to complete first. There actually wasn't enough space on the women's room counter for the number of concoctions to apply. After the five-step procedure of simple face washing, we had creams for night-time protection, revitalizing, resurfacing, skin-firming eye gels, lip plumps, and even the coveted wonder creme, Retin-A. The absurdity! Couldn't we skip even one night of application of these wrinkle creams? And what kind of example were we "older" women being for the "younger" women? Was this the discipline we should impart to Generation Next? How much more would be gained if they witnessed this discipline in our prayer life or Bible study? *WWJD?*

Jesus would discipline himself in what is eternal, certainly not pursue the temporal. He would also emphasize that the value of a man or woman is not what one sees on the outside of a person, but what beauty is found inside. I am praying I maintain a balance as I determine to grow old gracefully. Hopefully, I won't lose sight of the key element, *grace.*

It is difficult in this age of beauty to keep the focus on the heart, for this is where peace, contentment, and happiness can be found. As we all grow older, we must indeed think about the messages we pass along to our children and grandchildren. Do we want them to grow up thinking no one ever turns gray or has a few wrinkles? Or do we want them to see confident men and women who realize that their value is not in how they look, but rather how they act in the eyes of God.

—BC

SUPERNATURAL STRENGTH

I can do all things through Christ who strengthens me.
(Phil. 4:13)

As a Christian psychiatrist, I well know that God will *not* give us supernatural strength every time we ask for it. When my youngest son was five years old I took him to his first Superman movie. After the film my son prayed that God would give him the strength and abilities of Superman. Then, in total faith, he climbed up on a bench, tried to fly, and landed flat on his face.

It was a good lesson for him, and I politely told him so. Nevertheless, when I wasn't looking, he tried to fly at least two more times in the next ten minutes and fell flat on his face each time. He finally gave up.

But I do believe that during special trials and circumstances—when we really need it—God provides the amount of strength we need. And only He can determine how much we really *need* (not want) for that circumstance.

A few years ago, for example, I was driving our family in our van during a snowstorm, and, just ahead of us, a college girl's car slid into another car and then—smack—into a bridge abutment. She broke both legs, both arms, part of her face, and was semiconscious. It looked like her car might soon burst into flames. Someone ran to call an ambulance while a couple of men with a crowbar tried to pry her door open to get her out if the car exploded. They just couldn't get it open. As my car pulled up to the scene my mind raced wondering what I should do. The answer quickly came, *I'm a medical doctor and a Christian. I have to do whatever I can to save her life.*

So I jumped out of my car, ran over to hers, carefully broke her window with my hands, then grabbed the top of her door with my bare hands, bent the door down, then ripped it off its hinges. I told the frightened girl to pray and told her that she would be okay. We cut her seat belts off and put a blanket on her until the ambulance arrived a few seconds later. I followed up on her by phone at the hospital and have corresponded with her from time to time since then. She is doing fine now, but her recovery took months.

The crowd at the accident scene were rather stunned when I ripped the car door off with my bare hands. My family was too. There is no way I would have the strength to do that again right now. But at that moment, at the time that I prayed for God's help, at the moment I needed it, I had an adrenaline rush and the supernatural power of Christ to strengthen me.

Are you in a precarious situation right now? Ask yourself WWJD?, pray for strength, and realize that God may not give you as much strength as you want, but He will give you as much as you need.

—*PM*

A Tongue
Like Fire

*And the tongue is a fire, a world of iniquity . . . With it
we bless our God and Father, and with it we curse men,
who have been made in the similitude of God. Out of the
same mouth proceed blessing and cursing. My brethren,
these things ought not to be so. (James 3:6a,9–10)*

Children can be cruel. Kids shout at one another, fight,
and attempt to bully one another. I can still hear the
kids in my playground days poking fun, "Tommy and
Anna sittin' in a tree K-I-S-S-I-N-G" and so on. There were
many more lyrical torments, I'm sure you remember. Sometimes
it would be intentional hurt, and other times it was meant to
be a joke, but more often than not, this banter was at the
expense of someone's feelings. My own verbal cruelty taught
me a hard lesson that still haunts me.

Nine years old and in the fourth grade, I always rode the
bus to school in the morning. Our bus always arrived at school
about thirty minutes before classes actually started. The kids

were all shuffled into the cafeteria and told to sit down. Some kids would do their homework, and others, like me, would sit at the same table every morning and chat.

I always sat with the same group of girls. Some of us rode the bus together, and others were either dropped off by their parents or walked to school. One particular morning, one of my friends, Jasmine, and her little sister came in a little later than usual. There were six of us girls already seated and having a good time. Jasmine and her little sister came over and started to pull up a chair as they always did. However, that particular morning, the most hurtful, stupid, and mean-spirited thing that has ever come out of my mouth did. I looked up at Jasmine, waving my finger and said, "This table is reserved for whites only."

Shock and humiliation covered her face and her eyes began to well with tears. Even worse, her little sister started bawling frantically. How could I have been so cruel? Well, *What would Jesus do?* First, Jesus never spoke without clear judgment, which I obviously lacked as a nine year old. So He would have never been in my situation in the first place. The Bible tells us that when we are in the wrong, we are to be quick to admit our fault and apologize. When I finally realized what I had actually said, I immediately apologized to Jasmine and her little sister. Unfortunately it was too late, I had hurt Jasmine and her sister deeply.

Jasmine went over and told one of the teachers what I had said and my other friends all got up and left the table, each deservedly laying into me about how insensitive and mean I was. The teacher came over and gave me a few detentions and a good lecture. However, nothing was more humiliating for me than the punishment given by my friends. They temporarily banished me from the group.

I really never intended to hurt her; after all, she was my friend. To this very day, I don't know how, at the age of nine, I would have come up with such a slanderous statement. I never heard talk of bigotry at home or at school. I must have heard that line on television or in a movie, but that's still no excuse. I should have been more guarded with my speech.

Now as an adult, I work every day to guard my speech and be sensitive to other people's feelings. It was a lesson I'm glad I learned long ago, but I learned more than that from the incident. Proverbs 18:19 states, "A brother offended is harder to win than a strong city, / And contentions are like the bars of a castle." Although I received her forgiveness, we were never friends again. I didn't blame her; after all, who wants to be friends with someone who is hurtful toward you?

Someone once made up the saying, "Sticks and stones will break my bones, but words will never hurt me." I don't know what fool made up that rhyme. Bones will heal in time, but words are like fire that burn with sorrow and indignity.

Verbal cruelty often lingers into adulthood. Adults criticize with a humorous tone in order to mask the severity of the statement. This can be so hurtful. In the future, try to remind yourself WWJD? What words did Jesus deliver? He delivered words of kindness, friendship, encouragement, hope, healing, and forgiveness.

—HG

CONVICTION
VERSUS COMPROMISE

Esteeming the reproach of Christ greater riches than the
treasures in Egypt; for he looked to the reward.
(Heb. 11:26)

My husband and I have been in the Christian gift manufacturing business for more than twenty years. In the mid-eighties we were contacted by a local company interested in buying a unique-sized picture frame. Always eager for new business, my husband made an appointment to present various frames and prices to the potential customer. Arriving at the business, my husband grew excited about the opportunity that might result from this meeting. He entered the main lobby and was escorted to a large plush conference room with a highly polished walnut table surrounded by equally plush tufted leather chairs. Soon, three well-dressed men and one woman joined him, and the meeting began.

The meeting was going very well, the frame quantity was sizable, a frame style had been selected, and the numbers were being crunched and quickly approved. My husband saw dollar signs and was pleased that the meeting was going better than expected. He encountered no real challenges, no hard negotiations, very friendly people, and the potential for a long-term relationship.

The situation changed, however, when one of the group asked if we could recommend a company that could frame their picture and package it for shipping. My husband was thrilled when he thought all this company needed was an empty frame. He quickly stated, "We can do that." Within minutes the bottom line on the order grew and the final price was approved.

Finalizing details, my husband asked for a copy of the picture so he could take it back to the office and make a sample for their approval.

Within seconds, the excitement of this opportunity was stolen from him when they handed him a picture of a popular alcoholic beverage sitting on a table in a barroom setting, with a headline encouraging the reader to indulge.

His response to this image was instinctive. "I'm sorry, but let me recommend a company that can do this job for you. You see, we are a Christian company that makes gift products that share the good news and love of Jesus Christ."

With some additional explanation, and a complete testimony of my husband's faith, the group finally seemed to accept his reasons for not taking the job. After returning to our office, my husband began to second-guess his action. Was he being too harsh and judgmental? In the end, his decision was final, and my husband affirmed it when he said, "You don't make decisions based on circumstance, you make decisions based on principal."

About three months later, my husband received a call from the woman in the meeting. She explained that she had bought the company shortly after their meeting and now had several projects she would like for our company to do (not bid, but do)! She explained she respected my husband's convictions, admired his honesty and straightforwardness, and for those reasons, she knew she could trust him to be fair and honest in his dealings with her. Ultimately, the account grew and the overall result was far greater than ever projected.

Sometimes we must make sacrifices for Christ. It may be money, status, possessions, or even relationships, but it is better to make small, temporal sacrifices here on earth rather than compromise our cherished beliefs.

—BC

NUMBERED
DAYS

So teach us to number our days,
That we may gain a heart of wisdom.
(Ps. 90:12)

My dear, godly mother-in-law was reading Psalm 90 and 91 back on November 12, 1989. The verses about numbering your days, God being our refuge, and angels protecting us echoed over and over in her mind. She woke up that night with a bad dream—that one of her children or sons-in-law was involved in a car accident. She told no one about the dream but prayed every day that week for our protection.

On November 15, 1989 I was driving my car home from work, listening to the Bible on my car stereo like I usually do. That day, I happened to be listening to Psalm 66:10b–12, three of the strangest verses in the Bible: "You have refined us as silver is refined. / You brought us into the net; / You laid affliction on our backs. / You have caused men to ride over our heads; /

We went through fire and through water; / But You brought us out to rich fulfillment."

I stopped my tape as I was making a left turn at a major intersection, puzzled by the meaning of those unusual verses and *pow*! I was hit by an oncoming car I had pulled right in front of. The other car hit mine on the right front fender so hard that my car flew up in the air and flipped totally around, front to back while in the air, and landed on my roof. As it was spinning I was totally calm and thinking to myself, *So this is what God has in store for me today!* Both cars were totaled. Mine was folded like an accordion. I had my seat belt on so I was hanging upside down, an inch from the pavement. Neither driver was scratched. Men were literally flying over my head, like the Psalm said, and God laid affliction on my back and delivered me from the fire and steaming water of my burning car. I broke my window with my fist, took off my seat belt, crawled out (then stupidly crawled back in momentarily to get my cassette tape and my *Dallas Cowboy Weekly*,) then back out in time.

An ambulance came, but quickly left since no one was hurt. The policeman came just as the ambulance was leaving and asked me if the ambulance had just carried away "the body." He couldn't believe that I was "the body," standing without a scratch.

There is no doubt in my mind that God took sovereign action on my behalf that day. But if you still think all this was coincidence, read on.

Later, that very same night, I woke up with one of the very strong visions I occasionally have in my sleep. I call them "God dreams." Jesus was in my dream, telling me to get that Bible cassette tape I recovered from the car and listen to it until a verse "hit me between the eyes." I woke trembling because I felt the presence of God. I listened to the tape in my Walkman. Psalm 66, 67, but nothing "hit me between the eyes" until I got to Psalm 90:12—the verse about numbering our days to gain a heart of wisdom. I knew God was telling me to dedicate my life to Him one day at a time.

I had trusted Christ as my Savior at age six. I've been reading (or listening to) the Bible since I was ten—daily. And I dedicated my life to serve Christ as a physician at age sixteen. So I was already living for and serving God. But my life has never been the same since November 15, 1989, because I "reckoned myself dead unto Christ" that night and have considered every day since then a gift from God—a gift I now dedicate to Him every morning.

The next morning I found out about my mother-in-law's dream and daily prayer for me that week based on her "coincidental" dream, and on her study of Psalm 90:12, in which she felt God's Holy Spirit moving her heart to pray.

Absolutely amazing. The sovereignty of God in this incident is beyond doubt.

Now understanding that God has numbered my days, and wants me to live every day to the full and for Him, I diligently ask each day, What would Jesus do?

—*PM*

To Abstain or Not to Abstain?

For this is the will of God, your sanctification: that you should abstain from sexual immorality; that each of you should know how to possess his own vessel in sanctification and honor, not in passion of lust, like the Gentiles who do not know God. (1 Thess. 4:3–5)

I had to make a lot of tough choices growing up, and the older I got the more difficult the dilemmas. I believe one of the most difficult choices an individual has to make concerns sexual morality. Some adhere to God's standard, but sadly many—even Christians—ignore His request that we remain sexually pure.

Our society places so much importance on sex, sexual relationships, and the freedom to make your own choices. Even when the choices involve risking your health or your life, we are told we have the freedom, just be careful and enjoy. I'm sure it's not news to you. Our television, radio, and movies bombard us with these messages every single day.

As Christians, if we believe in God and if we believe He is our Creator, then we have to concur that God knows what is best for us. God knew what He was doing when He gave us sexual intimacy between two partners. He meant sex to be the deepest expression of love between one man and one woman in a covenant relationship established in the holiest of ceremonies before Him. God gave us His Word not to take away our freedom but to free us from the hurtful entanglements premarital sex can bring. God's Word is an outline for how we are to conduct our lives. What makes us think that any disobedience to His design could bring us any amount of pleasure or satisfaction beyond the moment?

What would Jesus do? During my dating relationships I had to ask myself that question over and over again in order to remind myself that my body is a temple of the Holy Spirit. To defile my body would be to defile the Holy Spirit. Jesus walked in our shoes for thirty-three years. He did not falter, not even once.

I know it's tough. My husband and I dated for four years before we were finally married. I'll be the first to admit there were times when we really struggled. We had to get up and walk away from each other for a while. We are only human; the desire to be intimate is constant. However, we had made a choice at the beginning of our relationship to not have sex before marriage. We knew it was not God's will for our relationship, at least not at that time.

We were finally married after four long years. Yes, it was worth the wait. Definitely. God has richly blessed our relationship because we chose to honor His will. One of the reasons I believe we have so many divorces in our country today is because of those who elect to continually build their relationships on the basis of lustful passions. If your relationship is only built on passion, what happens when the passion fades? By abstaining from sex, my husband and I were able to spend four years building a friendship that will stand the test of time. Someday, when the passion fades, we know our friendship will keep our love alive.

I think that even if I had not been a Christian I might have abstained from sex until marriage anyway. There are too many risks involved with premarital sex, especially for a female. Television and educators will give you statistics on the likelihood of getting pregnant, or the likelihood of contracting a disease, but who wants to be part of a likelihood. I don't believe the few seconds of glory are worth the risk. I believe there is no sex more gratifying, more intimate, or more loving, than the sexual intimacy between a husband and wife. Any sexual intimacy outside the confines of marriage is selfish love.

God was right to want sex to be restricted to marriage. Look at the mess our society is in because of it's lack of obedience in the flesh. We would have fewer divorces, fewer abortions, the spread of sexually transmitted diseases would cease if we only would adhere to sexual morality. Even an atheist could not deny its benefits.

Some of you may be reading this and saying, "What about me? I've already blown it." Well, that's where the grace of God comes in. If you confess your sins to the Lord, He promises to wash you clean again. One of my good friends faced the emotionally wrenching consequences premarital sex can bring. Our friendship suffered severely because being around another Christian only added to her guilt.

After about eighteen months, God broke her spirit, and I watched my friend go through deep hurt. It was during that time that her life in Christ was renewed, and for the first time, she truly experienced the incredible grace and forgiveness our God gives. Just last weekend I met with my friend and she told me that she has been amazed at God's forgiveness, and she feels totally new and refreshed again. I know He can do the same for you.

Resisting the bombardments of the media and intense momentary passion is incredibly difficult but certainly worthwhile and what Jesus would want us to do. If you are having difficulty in this area, meditate on God's Word, pray for guidance, and take comfort in His abundant grace.

—HG

BICYCLE AND
PENNY GENEROSITY

I have no greater joy than to hear that my children walk in truth. (3 John 4)

My dad gave my son, Cord, his first "grown-up" bike. Daddy always had the gift of recognizing quality, and this bike had all the bells and whistles that delight a little boy. He was careful to put it away at night and at other moments when not riding it, with one exception. One afternoon he left his beloved bike in the driveway for just a few minutes and when he returned, it was gone.

My husband decided that Cord could get another bike if Cord could raise half of the price of the bike. Though we would have loved to replace that bike for Cord, we felt he needed to learn a practical lesson about taking care of possessions. In time, Cord saved money from his allowances and chores and got another bike. It wasn't like the one his granddad had given him, but he was happy with it. This time around he brought the bike inside the house if he had to leave it for even a second.

Like cars, styles change, and two years later Cord longed for the newest popular bike style. That Christmas his dad delivered. Cord was thrilled. He wanted to ride it everywhere. We even transported it by car if the distance was too far to a friend's house.

One of Cord's best friends didn't have a bike. This wasn't obvious to Cord until he had two bikes. Realizing he could do something nice for his friend, Cord told his father he would like to give his other bike, the one he had helped pay for, to his friend. It really is true that there is no greater joy than seeing your children exhibit the Christian principles you try so hard to model at home. We were very proud of Cord that day.

Our daughter, J.J. also had a generous heart. Our children attended a Christian school that focused on various mission projects throughout the year. During junior high, her class targeted a family in need of some emergency funding. The evening after she found out about the family, J.J. stayed in her room longer than usual. When my husband and I investigated, we found her in the middle of her floor surrounded by piles of pennies. These were the pennies she had hoarded in a large jar in her room. J.J. explained that she had decided to roll all her pennies for the family in need. What did Mom and Dad do? Tried to maintain our composure as we sat down beside her to roll coins. The next day she carried her heavy load of sixty penny rolls into the classroom, knowing the meaning of cheerful giving.

The fruit of consistent parenting and modeling Christian principles are moments when our children surprise us and act Christlike of their own accord. Imagine how delighted God must be when He sees us follow the principles He modeled to us through His Son.

—BC

CONFORMED
TO THE IMAGE

For whom He foreknew, He also predestined to be
conformed to the image of His Son. (Rom. 8:29a)

After I had my life-changing car wreck on November 15, 1989, and my subsequent dream teaching me to dedicate my life to God one day at a time, this verse from Romans became very significant to me. The immature, selfish part of me has always wanted God to be my "supernatural genie in the sky" so I could play God and tell *Him* what to do. Well, if it worked that way I would be king of the world, a trillionaire (giving most of the money to missions, of course), and I would eat buttered popcorn all day without gaining weight. I would have no disease, perfect children, and perfect friends. Somewhere down the line, I would take care of world peace and all those other good things! Fortunately, God doesn't let me be "god" (for which you should be very thankful), and He refuses to be my genie.

God's goal for my life is actually for me to become more

and more like Christ, who came to earth to be a poor and humble servant and to give His life as a ransom for many. That means if my life is like His, I should expect even more car wrecks, diseases, setbacks, and disappointments. In fact, Jesus told us that the righteous should expect many afflictions.

So now, every morning I wake up and pray that God will make me more like His Son, Jesus, knowing full well that I am inviting suffering and tribulation to produce patience and other Christlike virtues in me. And tribulations came.

A few years after my car wreck, I had a dream that two of my boys and I were on a hill looking down on a large California highway. One of my daughters—I didn't know which one—was driving a car down that highway when, all of a sudden, her car stopped for no reason and another car rammed into the rear end of my daughter's car. Then an enormous cartoon ambulance came to the scene but skipped right over my daughter's car and kept going without helping her.

It was a very intense dream, so I took it more seriously than most of my dreams. In fact, the next morning I asked Jesus for wisdom and then called up my good friend, Dr. Robert Wise, with whom I had written a book on dreams, *Windows of the Soul* (Thomas Nelson Publishers, 1995). Robert agreed to pray for me and my children. He warned me that the dream may be a warning from God that there might be a shake-up in my business, but that hopefully no one would get hurt since no one was hurt in the dream despite the rear-end collision.

Later that very same day, my daughter Cheryl was driving

down a California highway and her brakes locked for no reason. An illegal alien (with no insurance) ran into the rear end of her car (and later sued her—after all, it was California). But no one was hurt. Later that week, one of my other boys (who wasn't in the dream) got into two car wrecks, neither of which was his fault. Both cars were totaled, but again, no one was hurt. And a little bit later that year, Robert's hunch came true. Some totally unexpected shake-ups occurred in my business that hurt and scared me at the time but worked together for good in the long run with no one "dying in the wreck."

On the day of my daughter's collision, she called me up on the phone (within the hour after the accident) and was pretty shaken. She was even more shocked when my wife and I told her about my dream the previous night and told her we had been praying for her at the time of her wreck. Both she and my son grew as a result of those car wrecks, as I did from my own car wreck in 1989. So through these tribulations, God guided us to pray and trust in His sovereignty. Through all of this, God's love, grace, and sovereignty never cease to amaze me.

I continue to pray that I will not be shaken off my foundation when these tribulations occur,

but rather that I will be shaken to trust Christ more and daily be further conformed to His image.

—PM

My
Pot of Gold

He who spares his rod hates his son,
But he who loves him disciplines him promptly.
(Prov. 13:24)

As a little girl, there was one thing in Daddy's closet that I coveted—his change pot. It was a large green pot in which he would throw his pocket change at the end of each day. After a while, he could amass over a hundred dollars in coins by just throwing his spare change in the pot.

I always got into trouble with that change pot. When I was three years old my parents were working out in the yard and I was playing. All of a sudden I heard the melodious and intoxicating music of the ice cream truck. I asked Mom and Daddy if I could have some money for ice cream on that hot Texas summer evening. Health conscious as my parents were, and dinner only being an hour away, I got a big, fat "No!"

Being a little devious, I came up with a brilliant little plan. I went back in the house, straight to Daddy's closet, and into the change pot, but I didn't pull out any change. Daddy had some cash in there. I took one of the bills and slipped out the back door. I was home free and on my way to the ice cream truck, or should I say, the ice cream meltdown.

My ten-year-old brother and his friend came around the corner and asked me where I was going. Although I was devious, I wasn't too smart. I told him I was on my way to the ice cream truck and Mom and Daddy had given me the money. My brother saw the bill in my hand and took it from me. He and his friend looked at it. No, it wasn't a one, no, it wasn't even a ten, it was a hundred dollar bill. My brother, Dwight, marched me right back to the house.

I never got my ice cream, but I got punished for being disobedient. You would think that I might have learned from that incident, but the saga continues.

As a second grader, there was nothing I detested more than eating the healthy lunch my mother so lovingly made for me each day. After all, all the other kids (so it seemed) got to buy their school lunches, which consisted of chocolate milk and Little Debbie snacks. I thought I had it all figured out. Each day I would sneak in to my daddy's closet and pull thirty or forty cents out so that I could buy a chocolate milk or a Little Debbie snack. My parents never noticed. However, one day I got greedy. That day at school they were serving a plate lunch special, ravioli. It was my favorite. So that morning I snuck into Daddy's closet and loaded my little purse up with all the change I could grab from his change pot.

That morning I was feeling a bit nervous carrying my load around, especially sitting next to my mother in the car on the way to school. Then, sure enough, I dropped my little purse on the floorboard of the car. "Ker-ching!" My mom picked up my purse and opened it to find my stolen goods. Can you say "grounded"? I was grounded for two whole weeks. No friends and no TV.

I know it must have been hard for my parents. I was so disobedient as a little child. As Christian parents, they struggled with spanking me and having to ground me. However, they did what was right. Our heavenly Father often rebukes us, but at the same time, He reaffirms His love for us. My parents modeled that. I now thank them for every grounding and spanking. They punished me, but then always reaffirmed their love for me. The discipline they gave provided a firm foundation for me to grow in respect for my parents, my heavenly Father, and to learn what is right from wrong.

Disciplining children is one of the most difficult things parents have to do. Can you imagine how difficult it must have been for God to punish His children, the Israelites? But the lessons learned from their forty years in the desert served their purpose and have been

passed down from generation to generation instructing millions of Jews and Christians. Remember that the discipline you mete out today may not only serve your child well, but may benefit your grandchildren and future generations as well.

—HG

Miss Astor

Do not lay up for yourselves treasures on earth, where moth and rust destroy and where thieves break in and steal. (Matt. 6:19)

When Satan wants to tempt me, he uses material possessions. I came from a family where Dad was the sole provider and money was tight. I don't know how, but he managed to raise three kids, support an alcoholic wife, and remain debt-free on his modest income. We lived very comfortably, and had the best clothes his Sears revolving charge account afforded. We always looked like we stepped out of the best fashion magazines. My dad wanted to give us the best he could, and he did. No matter what income we had, we cultivated high standards in all that we did. In high school I certainly wasn't the richest girl in class, but I could, however, pass for such with a little creativity and fashion flair and so my dad affectionately called me "Miss Astor." If you're familiar with America's affluent families, you may recognize that Mary Astor, in her day, achieved excellence in every area of her life and yet had a generous, giving nature. She was one of the greatest philanthropists of all time.

Having an innate love of and a surprising flair for fashion (surprising because I had grown up in small towns and had shopped only from Sears until I was seventeen), I devoured fashion magazines, biographies, television, and movies. I eventually left that small town, and went to the fashion mecca, Dallas, Texas, in 1966 as an Audrey Hepburn, Jacquelyn Kennedy, and Twiggy wanna-be. Oh, did I mention that I'm an optimist and a dreamer!

Well, dreams do come true, and at twenty-one I was married to a wonderful guy who had the ability to sell anything to anyone for anything. Commissions on that talent were lucrative, and as happened with many successful couples in the seventies and eighties, we considered our income highly disposable and accumulated many material things.

Five years after we married, my husband became a believer. and at the moment he made his decision for Christ, the Holy Spirit worked miraculously to help my husband get his priorities straight. One of the changes we saw was his lack of motivation to accumulate material possessions—for himself, anyway. Always having a generous nature, my husband developed the gift of giving. Over the next twenty-five years he gave away cars, refrigerators, washers, dryers, furniture, clothing, air travel, jewelry, sports equipment, and money. I've often thought, one day my husband will come home and tell me he has given away our home and everything in it. You might think I would be opposed to his disregard for material things given my bent toward things, but actually I'm not. I get as much pleasure from giving as he does. The difference between us lies in how I deal with my personal possessions. This is a constant battle between my old nature and new nature. My husband's hands are always open, giving whatever is needed, but if I focus on my own treasured possessions, I end up doing battle with the devil himself.

About twenty years ago the Lord decided to deal with this area of my life, to show me I shouldn't hold onto my things with a tight fist. My husband and I attended a marriage seminar where we focused on a new topic each week. We were then challenged to meditate and act on what we learned during the course of the following week. This particular week focused on material possessions. I knew I had a giving nature, but I was convicted about the value I placed on my own possessions. Through personal quiet time and prayer, one particular "treasure" kept coming into my thoughts.

One Christmas, my husband chose an exquisite ring for me that was delicately cast in a free-form gold mounting containing a single black pearl and diamond. It was incredibly beautiful, and I wore it all the time. Apart from my wedding rings, this was the most valuable piece of jewelry I owned. Before this moment I had never thought of parting with it, but somehow I knew that was exactly what God wanted me to do.

I was reluctant to tell my husband of my decision because I felt like I was giving a chunk of his heart away as he had chosen that ring just for me. But when I told my husband I felt I needed to do this he didn't question me at all. He was very supportive, loving, and proud of me. The Lord also showed me the woman who should have the ring and my husband agreed. She was so grateful. She also knew it was important to me that she not be reluctant to accept it. I saw her fifteen years later and she still had it on.

I never regretted giving her the ring. The Lord changed my heart during that time and now I keep these words from Matthew 6:21 as a constant prayer, "For where your treasure is there your heart will be also."

I still appreciate beautiful things, but now I'm content not to acquire them and just to let them belong to others. God knows my heart, and it pleases Him when I regard my earthly treasures with open hands. I also like to think my dad would say, "Well done, Miss Astor."

Where do you store your treasures? Treasures are not just material possessions. Perhaps you focus too much on career, prestige, or power. All of these things are temporal treasures and will all die away eventually. What truly brings joy are

the eternal treasures of service to God and relationships with family and friends.

—BC

Career Choices

But seek first the kingdom of God and His righteousness,
and all these things shall be added to you. (Matt. 6:33)

Making life choices is difficult enough when your choices are limited by education or economic considerations. My education was, fortunately for me, diverse and extensive. After college, I pursued a master's degree in cardiovascular physiology, then an M.D., and then finished a psychiatry residency mentored by Dr. Bill Wilson at Duke University Medical School. I was thirty years old when I finished my primary professional training. I continued in school for the next decade, finally getting a seminary degree from Dallas Theological Seminary when I was forty years old. So when I finished my psychiatric training at Duke at age thirty, I had a big career choice to make.

Where should I go? What type of psychiatric practice should I have? With whom? How could I best use the talents and education with which God had blessed me? My wife, Jan, and I already had three children and great debts from my thirteen years of education. I had two excellent job offers for more than $100,000 per year and was thrilled! (Remember this was 1975! Most psychiatrists actually earn much less than that now due to the changes in our insurance system.) I prayed, *Thank you, God, for calling me into psychiatry!* But, just to make sure I was heading in the right direction, I asked myself and God, *What would Jesus do?*

Well, as Jesus sometimes prompts us to do, I felt led to do a little research before making a final decision about my job offers. I needed to find out how my particular set of talents could best be used to further God's kingdom. I found out that most of the counseling in America back in 1975 was done by pastors, priests, and rabbis, and that most of them had very little training in counseling. God definitely convicted me that I could probably do more good training pastors in counseling than just practicing psychiatry on a few thousand patients in my lifetime.

So, I called Trinity Evangelical Divinity School in the Chicago area to see if they had any interest at all in hiring a psychiatrist to teach their future pastors. The administrative secretaries gave me the home phone number of Dr. Ken Kantzer, the academic dean at the time. I called him immediately and Dr. Kantzer, a man of deep faith, told me that he was on his knees praying for a psychiatrist when the phone just rang. He felt like it was a divine coincidence, invited me for a job interview, and then hired me. I had a wonderful experience there teaching for a year and a half, but then felt led to go and teach at Dallas Theological Seminary where they did not yet have any psychology teachers.

I taught full-time at Dallas for a dozen years for a starting salary of $12,600 per year, a big step down from the $100,000 job offers I had turned down in private practice after my graduation. God was faithful and clearly had other plans for me and my family. Wonderful things happened as a result of our putting God first and acting on *WWJD?*

First, God gave me some excellent students to influence and train, including Dr. Tony Evans, Dr. John Townsend, Dr. Henry Cloud, Dr. John Trent, Dr. David Biebel, and many others. What a blessing to be able to influence the lives of these godly men and women and put this opportunity above money.

Second, God led me to write many books because there were no Christian psychology texts to teach from when I began my work. I've written about two books per year, more than fifty now, and several of them have sold close to one million copies each.

Third, God led me into further professional growth. This included opportunities in daily Christian radio—bringing the principles of psychology founded in the Word of God to millions of listeners in the comfort of their homes—and as the medical director of the New Life Clinics—Christ-centered facilities for intensive psychological discovery and healing.

Thank you, Dr. Ken Kantzer, for being on your knees praying for a psychiatrist to teach pastors twenty-three years ago.

Following Christ is often relegated to Sunday mornings and during daily devotions. But Jesus wants us to ask WWJD? with the most fundamental questions in our lives including what our jobs should be. To start, consider your talents, skills, and experience, and then consider the needs of the kingdom of God and see where these areas overlap. Seeking first the kingdom of God may not mean making a radical job change, but it may mean making a radical attitude change.

—PM

WELL DONE, MY GOOD AND FAITHFUL SERVANT

Well done, good and faithful servant; you have been faithful over a few things, I will make you ruler over many things. Enter into the joy of your lord. (Matt. 25:23)

When I was in college I had the pleasure of working with my church's senior high school group. It was so much fun. I enjoyed being with the kids, and we always did a lot of neat activities together. The most fun was our annual spring break ski trip. The group would rent big passenger vans to make the trek to Colorado. Our youth pastor thought the forced togetherness would facilitate what we affectionately called bonding, and he was right.

I remember a conversation I had with one of the kids on one particular trip. He and I contemplated theology, the way we live our lives, and how best to serve the Lord. I have to admit, this kid showed a lot of maturity. He hit me with a statement that still affects me. He said, "When I die, I can't think of anything more amazing than to have the God of the universe look at me and say 'Well done.'" I sat there stunned. Honestly, the thought had never crossed my mind before.

Ever since that conversation I, at times, think about exactly what it would take for God to look at me and say, "Well done." How would I need to live my life? I'm not a missionary, a pastor, or any great theologian. How is it, that as an ordinary individual leading an ordinary life, I could do anything that would be so deserving of a "Well done." For instance, when I compare my life to Mother Teresa's, I feel ashamed that I have not accomplished enough for the glory of His kingdom. Even though I have given my life to Him, I haven't devoted my life to His service, or have I?

Last summer I had the wonderful opportunity to hear Elisabeth Elliot speak. During the course of the program she had women write down questions that she would answer at the end of the evening. One question really stuck with me. By the sound of it, the question came from a tired housewife who was dissatisfied with the mundane task of running a household and taking care of her children. To paraphrase her question, "I want to do more to serve the Lord, but my time is so consumed by the daunting tasks of cooking, cleaning, and taking care of my husband and our children. Where do I find the time? Is there any advice or encouragement you can give me?"

Ms. Elliot answered, "My dear lady, all the things that you do each and every day are for the glory of God. The sacrifices you make for your husband and your children are well-noted by the Lord. The Bible says that we can serve the

Lord in all that we do. By ironing your husband's shirt, cleaning up after your children, or more importantly, spending quality time with them, your faithfulness to these things is well-pleasing to Him who called you to do so. Therefore, I would venture to say you are already serving the Lord in many ways."

Wow! It was then that I understood what it means to receive a "Well done." *WWJD?* Jesus lived a life of faithfulness. In all that Jesus did, He was faithful to His family, His friends, His work, His people, and most of all, to the Father. What I've learned is that it doesn't matter what you do in life, so long as you do it with a sincere and worshipful heart.

If we live our lives with faithfulness to what God has called us to do, we will have many rewards waiting for us in heaven. Colossians 3:23–24 says, "And whatever you do, do it heartily, as to the Lord and not to men, knowing that from the Lord you will receive the reward of the inheritance; for you serve the Lord Christ." Well done, my good and faithful servant.

—HG

Point Blank

The LORD is my light and my salvation;
Whom shall I fear?
The LORD is the strength of my life;
Of whom shall I be afraid? (Ps. 27:1)

One evening my husband was out of town and my young children were tucked away for the night. A disgruntled friend, "under the influence," showed up at my front door demanding to be let inside. He felt I had somehow interfered in his personal life. On this night he was too angry to reason with, and, to make matters worse, he was holding a gun!

I was afraid to call my neighbors or the police, thinking this might provoke him further and then someone else might get hurt. But if I didn't open the door soon he would likely wake the kids, not to mention the neighborhood. As I spoke to him through the door I felt certain that if I didn't let him in, he would fire his gun through the door anyway.

This man had never been angry at me before. In fact, I think he even respected my Christianity. I always thought he desired to have the same relationship with God that I did, but was holding himself prisoner of other choices.

While standing at the door, I pleaded silently with God to help me know what to do, to protect everyone from harm, and to please let the kids sleep through this. Though it may be hard to believe, I really wasn't afraid for myself. Well, I opened the door and let him in.

Once inside, the verbal confrontation was even more harsh. So upset about what he perceived as my interference and challenging my attempts to calm him down, he kept yelling, "I can do anything I please and you can't stop me!" All through his ravings he was waving that gun.

I can remember everything he said to me, but I can't remember everything I said to him. God took over that night and gave me words to speak and angels to protect. I do remember speaking softly, trying not to wake the children. And I remember being afraid that this man would go looking for the kids. Maybe I could calm him if I remained calm myself. I was standing toe-to-toe with the devil that night; his eyes were fixed on mine hoping to make me tremble with fear. Continuing his verbal assault, this man threatened to kill me, not then, but if I ever tried to interfere again.

I stood firm. Maintaining calm and speaking softly, I do recall mentioning God and love in my words to him. Eventually, he backed down and left. I'm not so naive to think every time we face evil as Christians we can overcome physical harm or death, but I do have the confidence of Romans 8:31, no matter the outcome, "What then shall we say to these things? If God is for us, who can be against us?"

I don't know if Jesus would have opened the door in my situation, but I know that two thousand years ago He faced His enemies with confidence and love even unto death. What Jesus wanted me to do, and what I did, was to fervently pray for protection, to maintain the peace and calm of the righteous even in this desperate circumstance, and to trust my instinct, which I felt was God's direction for me at that moment.

It is easy and understandable to lose one's head and be overcome with fear in a life-threatening circumstance. But this is exactly why God has given us words of peace and strength to memorize, hold in our hearts, and take comfort when facing fear.

—BC

GREED

Your gold and silver are corroded, and their corrosion will
be a witness against you and will eat your flesh like fire.
You have heaped up treasure in the last days. (James 5:3)

Sometimes we ask *What would Jesus do?* and make good
decisions. Sometimes we ask and then choose to go
against Christian principles and make bad decisions. I
have made some really lousy decisions in my life. In my story,
"Career Choices," I mentioned turning down job offers with
salaries of more than $100,000 per year back in 1975 to instead
teach and mentor seminary students for $12,600 per year. This
was, in hindsight, a really good decision.

One of the outgrowths of this decision was my secondary
career as an author. I wrote books for good motives, to use as
textbooks for my seminary courses, and to help people. I was
honestly surprised when the books sold hundreds of thousands
of copies — pleasantly surprised! I ended up making a lot of
money and thinking, *Since I put the kingdom first, God must*

now be blessing my socks off! I must be justified, then, in living "high off the hog." I bought houses and condominiums, I overindulged my children, and I put all my earnings into a "Christian investment group." (Bankers call these "dumb doctor deals!")

Now, don't misunderstand me. There is nothing inherently wrong with being rich. In fact, God made some of the godliest men in the Bible also among the richest on earth: Abraham, Isaac, Jacob, Job, David, Solomon. It was Solomon who taught us in Ecclesiastes that if God makes us rich, we should enjoy it, but not live for it (5:18–20). There must be balance. I believed I was living for God and doing many good deeds, but I was actually tipping way off balance, beginning to obsess about money. So God took it all away.

In the eighties the real estate market crashed. Since I had signed on as a guarantor on a bunch of real estate loans through my investment group, when the group went under, I got stuck with millions of dollars worth of loans. I considered bankruptcy but then decided Jesus would have me try to pay off the debts, even if it took me the rest of my life (and it might!). God got my attention.

A dozen years have gone by since then. I now have a modest house and car. I'm able to help my kids through college and can afford to go on two or three foreign medical mission trips each year, but I own nothing else and I'm still working my way out of debt. But I'm happier and more content now than I've ever been because God improved my attitude. The

Lord gave, and the Lord has taken away. Blessed be the name of the Lord (Job 1:21b).

How many times and in how many ways must God tell us to be careful with money and not to put too much emphasis on it? It took a drastic action on God's part to help me finally realize what place money should have in my life. How would Jesus have you handle your own finances?

—PM

Do I Really
Need That?

My flesh and my heart fail;
But God is the strength of my heart
and my portion forever. (Ps. 73:26)

Have you ever wanted something so badly that you would justify any means necessary to get your hands on it? I know I have. I would venture to say that most of us have felt this way at one time or another. When I was twelve years old I wanted a pair of Guess overalls. I begged and pleaded with my mom, "If I could just get a pair of those Guess overalls I would be content; life would be great." My mom finally let me have my way.

It went on from there. When I was thirteen I wanted a Miata twenty-one-speed bicycle. After all, my best friend had one, and we wanted to be able to go places during the summer. It would be my only mode of transportation besides my feet. Once again, I knew I would be content if I just could get that bicycle. Well, Daddy gave in and bought me the bicycle.

When I was fourteen I wanted a Honda Elite 50 moped. I knew my world would be complete if I just could have that speedier mode of transportation. Once again, I got it and life was great, but only for a while. When I turned sixteen I begged and pleaded for a car. (I was an expert by now.) I just "needed" one so bad. Once again, I got my wish and life was super. Good-bye moped, hello automobile!

This saga of never ending wants continued. As I went through college, I realized something about myself. I had developed a very unhealthy pattern in my life. Looking back on all these things that I had to have (and there were many more I didn't mention), I was only satisfied with my new toy for a short time before I started to covet something else. I asked, "Why is it, that every time I receive something I want, I quickly tire of it and want something else?" Even though I was truly thankful for everything I had, it was never enough.

Materialism is like a disease. Unless you cut it off at the source, it just continues to grow and feed. I have to be honest, I still struggle with it to this day. Society suggests that instant gratification is the source of happiness. What I am finding is that instant gratification is the source of misery. As you get older your material wants grow in number and expense. You eventually reach a point where your income can't keep up with all of your desires and you make yourself miserable trying. At times I would almost get depressed because I didn't have the means to buy the things that I really wanted.

Well, *WWJD?* I had to give my "wants" over to Him and

ask Him to fill me with what I really needed in my life. If you take a deeper look at the life of Christ, you don't find thousands of acres, tons of gold and silver, fancy clothing, or a big house with servants. Christ himself was a servant, a simple man, a carpenter, a son, and a friend. His desires were bound up in things of eternal value, primarily the relationship He had with the Father and the relationships He had with his earthly family and friends. It finally hit me that I was already richly blessed with everything I needed.

I am finally surrendering to the fact that little else in this life matters than the simple blessings of His grace. How blessed I am to have a loving husband and family, to have a roof over my head, a bed to sleep in, food to eat, health, and most importantly, salvation through Christ. I thank Him for all these things every night as I go to bed. There is nothing I need any more than that. "And the world is passing away, and the lust of it; but he who does the will of God abides forever" (1 John 2:17).

Many of us run on empty. We try to feed our egos and sense of worth by accumulating as many things that show wealth as we possibly can. As Christians, our contentment should come from serving the Lord and daily spending time with our Father. Everyday, simple

obedience to the Father will gain riches for us in heaven that are far beyond our comprehension. As Christians, we need not look for what the world holds for us, but rather what we can bring to it.

—HG

DOC'S Z

Therefore, as we have opportunity, let us do good to all,
especially to those who are of the household of faith.
(Gal. 6:10)

Sometimes, helping others in need really takes us out of our comfort zone. One particular instance stands out so clearly to me, it might have happened just yesterday instead of thirteen years ago.

Our friends Rich and Patty and my husband and I were asked to help a woman in need. She relied on welfare and benevolent fellow believers for medical needs and everyday chores because she was housebound and confined to a wheelchair. We had been told others were helping her by bringing her meals and doing some household chores. Some people had been able to provide transportation to take her to the doctor or do her shopping. We were under the impression that our tasks would be similar, take her groceries, put them away, do some light housework, and she would be settled until the next volunteers arrived on their assigned day. We weren't prepared for what awaited us.

We arrived with groceries and entered the dark, musty, muggy front room of this woman's apartment. The air was stale from lack of air conditioning—she left the lights and window air unit off to conserve on her electric bill. Unpacked boxes were stacked strategically to allow her wheelchair access to the various apartment doors. The boxes contained what she had accumulated in her forty-plus years of living. She frequently lost her lease, so boxes were just moved from one apartment to the next. To add insult to injury, her husband left her and her two children when she became ill. Her children weren't there that day. I want to think they helped their mother when they could, but life must have been as despairing for her eight- and thirteen-year-old children as it was for her.

She had a bad spell that week and had not been out of her bed for days. Her room smelled of sickness, unwashed clothes, and bed linens. Every surface in the house was either coated in dust or sticky substances of unknown origin. Where to start?

We obviously were unprepared for the task before us. We had brought only the basic cleaning supplies. Assessing the necessity for more supplies, and her need for more groceries we sent the guys to the store. Patty and I started gathering laundry, stacking dirty dishes, and organizing the clutter. The minute we opened the drapes and blinds, roaches scurried to find dark places to hide. No, I'm not exaggerating. Maybe we were misinformed about how much others before us had helped her, but it didn't matter, God had put us here so *WWJD?* Everything He could.

The vacuum had to be emptied frequently. Floors and countertops required more than just a "once over." We had to change our friend's clothes and bed linens. She was a little defensive, and we were sensitive to our intrusion of her space. Maybe the others who had come before us gave up and left faced with the futility of their efforts.

Well, Jesus would do what He could so we did too. We worked until dark that day and left knowing we would police others' efforts to help her in the future. There was no good reason the Christian community involved in her life should work halfheartedly. Patty was so committed to our effort that she gathered all of this woman's laundry (the apartment's facilities couldn't possibly accommodate all the washing we needed to do) and offered to take it home, wash it, and bring it back the next day. Her husband's car would serve as the delivery truck.

Rich has owned a wonderful classic 280Z sports car as long as I've known him. It is red and fast. Rich's license tag bears the name DOC'S Z. (He's a veterinarian.) So, we loaded the hatchback of Rich's car with pillowcases full of dirty clothes. After pulling into their garage Patty and Rich unloaded their cargo. The next morning, Rich began to pull away from his garage but then stopped suddenly. He yelled for Patty. In the years since, the vision of the horror on Rich's face and in his voice has become a great inside joke between the four of us. The source of his horror? DOC'S Z was infested with roaches! *What would Jesus do?* Well Jesus encountered poverty, lepers, the blind, the crippled, the deranged, thieves, and prostitutes; the least we could endure were a few roaches.

Living a Christian life means getting involved and doing all tasks thoroughly and well so our service will be pleasing to God. There are so many people who need our care and commitment. Look today for some way to help out your community and your brothers and sisters in Christ. "And let us not grow weary while doing good, for in due season we shall reap if we do not lose heart" (Gal. 6:9).

—BC

Mentors

To Timothy, a true son in the faith. (1 Tim. 1:2a)

The apostle Paul was Timothy's mentor, exhorting and encouraging him like he would his own son. A unique relationship, and incredibly valuable to both people involved, mentoring basically involves teaching biblical principles and then getting personally involved to make sure one's charge follows through in adopting these principles.

Over the years I have been greatly blessed to have had many mentors at various stages in my life. These have included my own parents, my big brother, Dr. Richard Meier, Dr. Bob Schindler, all of my pastors, Dr. Ken Kantzer at Trinity Evangelical Divinity School, Dr. Haddon Robinson at Dallas Theological Seminary, and even some former students who now advise and encourage me in many ways, such as Drs. Henry Cloud and John Townsend.

In the early seventies I began my psychiatric training at the University of Arkansas Medical School. Though I had many excellent professors there, I longed to learn how to integrate the spiritual, emotional, and physical aspects of man. I had heard about an outstanding Christian psychiatrist at Duke University Medical School, Dr. William P. Wilson, who had published more than one hundred and fifty research articles on psychiatry, neurology, and even electroencephalography (EEGs). He was a scientist's scientist. And yet I heard that furthering the kingdom of Christ was his primary focus and heart's desire. In the seventies, Dr. Paul Tournier was the foremost Christian psychiatrist in Europe and Dr. Bill Wilson was the foremost Christian psychiatrist in America.

I knew Dr. Wilson must be extremely busy and assumed he wouldn't have time to take a phone call from a psychiatry resident in Arkansas, but one day I got up my courage and called him up. He shocked me. He was warm, personable, and even excited about what I was doing. Within a week or so, my wife and I were staying in his home as his houseguests, interviewing at Duke, and ultimately accepting his offer to come study with him at Duke. When I began my schooling at Duke I found out that Dr. Wilson had taken many Christian residents under his wing, including one who is now my prayer partner, Dr. David Larson, president of the National Institute of Health Research in Washington, D.C.

Dr. Wilson has been, and continues to be, a fatherly inspiration to me. He taught me not only psychiatry, but also spirituality and how to mentor others. One of the ways Dr. Wilson lived out *WWJD?* was to be this strong and consistent mentor for so many young men and women in the growing field of psychiatry.

Every believer has unique gifts and abilities to share with someone as a mentor. Though professional encouragement is important, the most helpful way you can mentor someone is to encourage them in their walk with the Lord. Remember the ninety-year-old widow in my church who encouraged me and prayed for me daily until she went to be with God? She was also my mentor. Ask God if He would have you enter into a mentoring relationship with someone, either as the mentor or "mentee"—you will be richly blessed.

—PM

THE DATING DILEMMA

Do not be unequally yoked together with unbelievers. For what fellowship has righteousness with lawlessness? And what communion has light with darkness? (2 Cor. 6:14)

It was a new and exciting year for me as I finally moved away from home and transferred from Richland Community College to the University of North Texas. Meeting new people and making new friends was a welcome change.

During the spring semester, a friend and I were working in the computer lab. There my friend introduced me to a really great guy who happened to be on the track team with her. He was six feet, two inches tall and had a great muscular build—the stereotypical college athlete. John had come to the United States from Ireland on a track and field scholarship. You know what a sucker women are for foreign accents.

That evening he asked for my phone number, and I happily gave it to him. I went back home with my friend and thought to myself, "That guy won't ever call." But, sure enough, about a week passed and just when I had forgotten about him, he called to ask me out on a date. Needless to say, I immediately accepted.

Our first date was wonderful. We had so much fun that we decided to go out again. One thing led to another, and within a few weeks we were an item. Since I hadn't dated too much before college, building a serious relationship was a new and exciting venture for me.

Four months passed, and we were growing closer every day. However, as we grew closer, I began to recognize something that I knew would be a potential problem if we were to fall in love deeply enough that we wanted to marry. Even though he had good moral standards for dating and had a religious background, John had never dedicated his life to Christ. Every time I brought up the subject, he changed it to something else.

I knew we were not "equally yoked" and had to ask myself, *What are my standards for a godly husband?* In dating, I have always believed that it is crucial to recognize whether or not your relationship can be a Christ-centered one. In this case I knew what Jesus would have me do, and I knew what I had to do before I got in way over my head.

Painfully, at the start of the fall semester, I broke things off with him. It was such a hard thing to do. I really liked going out with him, and I treasured his friendship. Essentially, this guy had everything going for him. However, I knew in my heart I couldn't pursue the relationship any longer. Missionary dating was not the answer. That fall semester, I decided I would pray that someone else would come into his life to share the saving grace of Jesus with him.

The semester went by, and I still saw him from time to time. At the end of the semester we saw each other a little more just as friends. I noticed that he was no longer that same proud and cocky guy. Despite a winning cross-country running season, somehow this guy had been humbled.

The end of the semester came, and he went home to Ireland for four weeks to be with his family. I continued to pray for him and sent him a Christmas care package. When school started up again we finally had that deep conversation I had been wishing for all along. He shared with me that during the fall semester he had been involved in a Bible study with Campus Crusade for Christ and that he had dedicated his life to the Lord at the end of October. You can't begin to imagine my excitement about how God had answered my prayers.

Three and a half more years passed, and that great guy became my husband. I have been richly blessed by God through him. What would have happened if I hadn't broken off my relationship with John? I will never know, but it is entirely possible that our relationship would have suffered deeply. Though it was hard at the time, I am now so glad I let go and let God.

Breaking off a relationship is never easy, especially when you still care about that person. But God is clear in His desire that we not be unequally yoked. Stories abound of spouses torn apart by their partner's unbelief. Although my story had a happy ending, some don't. But following God's Word would have been the right thing to do even if John and I didn't marry. WWJD? Jesus would have us follow His direction and trust that He will partner us with the perfect man or woman in the fullness of His time.

—HG

CUTTING WEIGHT
TO WIN

And you, fathers, do not provoke your children to wrath,
but bring them up in the training and admonition of the
Lord. (Eph. 6:4)

Westling is an unusual sport. While athletes in other sports try to bulk up to increase their power and strength, wrestlers try to gain an advantage by losing weight and competing with other men in a lower weight class. This practice is called cutting weight. At the end of 1997 three college wrestlers died from cutting weight to win. As I watched the grief-stricken parents testify about their children's tragic deaths on television, I recalled a painful episode in the wrestling career of our son, Cord.

Cord's sport of choice is wrestling. He began wrestling in the seventh grade and continued through his senior year in high school. My husband never missed a match. At Cord's graduation, he gave him a photo album of fifteen hundred pictures my husband had taken of Cord during his career.

There are still hundreds more pictures in our photo files that didn't make the cut for the album. I attended the matches, too, but the only way I could watch Cord when he was actually on the mat was through the lens of a video camera. Sometimes I would even glance away from the one-inch black-and-white viewing window because it was too painful for me to watch. There are many shots in our video library of gym floors, ceilings, or spectator's backsides because I looked elsewhere.

Cord was very good. One year he was a state champion. He seldom lost, and when he did, it was abhorrent to him. To me, wrestling seems lonely. You cannot rely on the rest of the players to bring you through a match. The wrestler faces the challenger alone, one-on-one. I never heard Cord put it in these words, but I imagine the adrenaline rush is a mix of ultimate victory and sheer terror. That's how I felt anyway.

Cord is a champion. Foremost in every champion's mind is to improve his game. During his junior year in high school he was victorious in the 125-pound weight class. This may sound like little weight to you. I guess it was, but in theory, if an older wrestler can lower his weight and maintain his strength, his experience usually "outweighs" his younger opponent in the same weight class. So when Cord reached his senior year, he decided to lose "just a few" pounds, and take his strength and experience to the 119-pound weight class.

I wasn't very happy with this theory. In my eyes and according to my home medical reference book, my son had matured to a five-foot, ten-inch young adult who had the body frame to support a minimum of 135 pounds.

This was one of those times when both parties felt they were right. Mother and son were both right. The son knew "his own self" and the mother knew "his own self." Cord had the discipline and determination to do whatever he thought he should do, and I knew Cord would do exactly that no matter the difficulty or sacrifice.

Wrestlers in high school had many tricks to cut weight. Cord skipped meals even when his coach advised against it. He soon learned this would cost him strength, so he just started watching what he ate. But this wasn't good enough for me. Cord consented to consult with our family physician to see if he was hurting himself. Our doctor ran the right tests, determining that Cord was still healthy. For you body fat enthusiasts, he had only 3 percent. Imagine! The doctor said, however, if he insisted on maintaining this physical stress he should consult with a nutritionist and do it the right way. He did. He thought this would make me happy. It did—to a point. He drank the right nutritional drinks, and ate the right foods to maintain strength and lean muscle mass. However, like other wrestlers, he went back to the extreme measures to make a weigh-in. These weigh-ins could occur twenty-four hours before or the day of a match.

He wore workout clothing that made him sweat. He would sit in saunas to make himself sweat. He would do rigorous exercise like jumping rope nonstop for long periods of time and then, instead of replenishing a sweaty body with fluids, he would spit any remaining saliva into a cup. What's a mother to do?

I don't know what Jesus would have done. Scripture tells us in 1 Timothy 4:8 that bodily exercise profits only a little, but in 1 Corinthians 9:24–27, Paul teaches a pattern for self-denial. Of course, he is referring to self-denial for the purpose of godliness, but the practical application of the analogy of an athlete can be applied by an athlete to his daily life. "Do you not know that those who run in a race all run, but one receives the prize? Run in such a way that you may obtain it. And everyone who competes for the prize is temperate in all things . . . I discipline my body and bring it into subjection, lest, when I have preached to others, I myself should become disqualified."

Cord measured "temperate in all things" differently than I measured "temperate in all things." If Cord erred in extreme bodily discipline, I erred in the discipline not to nag.

I nagged constantly. I cried, I ranted, I raved, I begged. Even though I had been reassured by medicine he was all right, I felt Cord was still at risk. Then one night the pressure I was putting on him hit its peak and provoked him to anger.

Cord had come in from working out and, as was his custom, he headed to the shower in our master bathroom. I was at it again through the locked bathroom door. Cord pleaded with me again to stop with the nagging, that he was fine. But

I persisted until I heard his fist go through one of the closet doors. There was silence. Then Cord said, "Mom, please don't say another word. Please."

I was full of remorse. I had driven him to this. On my side of the door, the sound of his fist was as clear as if God had spoken out loud. I had blown it. Thinking that Cord had spent his pent up frustration with that blow to the door, I opened my mouth to apologize and Cord's fist went through the other closet door. I silently left my side of the door. Cord had his shower, dressed, and left the house. My daughter was the one who found the fist holes in the doors. How awful for all of us. "Fathers, do not provoke your children, lest they become discouraged" (Col. 3:21.)

The doors were easily mended with some picture frames hung strategically over the holes. I was afraid what might not be so easily mended was Cord's spirit. Whether or not he was wrong in cutting his weight, I knew I was wrong in the way I handled it.

Well, love is spoken in our house. Every night since elementary school and even now when he is home as an adult, Cord will peek into our room saying, "Goodnight, Dad, I love you" and "Goodnight, Mom, I love you." That night when he came in, he said the same thing except he added, "I'm sorry, Mom." In an instant we were in each others arms holding tight.

Cord won his state championship at the 119-pound weight,

but mother and son had learned hard life lessons that final season. We were even closer after that painful time.

Sometimes the instructions Jesus gives us are as obvious and familiar as the fingers on our hands, yet aren't heeded until we, like me, hear a fist go through the closet door. When dealing with children, we must find constructive and age-appropriate ways to teach and discipline, respecting their God-given independence and intelligence all the while. We simply must not provoke them or we risk damage much greater than a few holes in a closet door.

—BC

FIGHTING
DEMONS

*For we do not wrestle against flesh and blood, but against
principalities, against powers, against the rulers of the
darkness of this age, against spiritual hosts of wickedness
in the heavenly places. (Eph. 6:12)*

My first actual missionary journey to a foreign country took place in 1985. I was the team physician for the Probe Ministries group that joined astronaut Jim Irwin's team to climb Mount Ararat in Turkey hoping to reveal Noah's ark to the world. U.S. reconnaissance photos have shown a large rectangular object in the ice that may be the ark.

While in Turkey I witnessed to many Moslems with no success. For some unknown reason, everyone on the team got permission to climb Mount Ararat except me. My permission was delayed. So my team went two-thirds of the way up the mountain without me, planning to wait a few days for me to join them while they got acclimated to the twelve-thousand-foot elevation.

Alone in my hotel at the foot of the mountain, I planned to climb the mountain the next morning with my guide. (I finally got my permit.) I woke up around 11:30 P.M., looked out my window with my binoculars toward the top of the mountain, and saw a bonfire in the distance. I assumed it was my team warming up, so I went back to sleep. In reality, Kurdish rebels had stolen my team's tents and supplies and were burning them with a large fire. The Kurds lined my teammates up in a firing line and said, "Ready, aim, fire" but didn't shoot. Instead, they sent my friends running down the mountain.

Not knowing any of this, I fell asleep that night but woke up at about midnight with an intense nightmare. I felt a demonic presence in the room—the only time in my whole life I have ever had that experience. I grabbed my mountain knife, sat on my bed praying for God's help in this spiritual battle, and prayed for protection for me and my team. I demanded out loud that any demons leave in the name of Jesus, and suddenly my window broke *from the inside out*. Suddenly I felt totally at peace and went back to sleep. The next morning I was preparing to climb Mount Ararat with my soldier guide when two of my team members entered the hotel totally fatigued, having run all night long down the mountain.

I don't know why I initially grabbed my mountain knife when I felt that demonic presence. It was really a silly thing to do—after all, can you imagine swishing a knife back and forth at a spiritual being? But when I asked Jesus what to do, I commanded the presence to leave in the name of Jesus Christ and, as I said, my third floor window broke from the inside out, landing on the porch outside my window.

Turkish soldiers went up the mountain and shot and killed the Kurdish rebels. Later, Jim Irwin and his team went up with John McIntosh from our group, who used my equipment, since everyone else's was burned in the fire. But the Turkish soldier wouldn't let Jim's team go to the site where we had determined the ark was located, possibly because the Moslem bible (the Koran) teaches that Noah's ark landed on nearby Mount El Judy, rather than on Ararat. Or possibly because Turkey is affiliated with NATO and may have missiles near that part of the northeast face of Mount Ararat, facing Russia and only a few miles from the point where Russia, Iraq, and Iran all meet.

I now believe demons on Mount Ararat inspired the rebels to chase my team away from the ark. Demons may also have inspired the Turks to kill those rebels and then to keep our team and astronaut Jim Irwin's team away from the ark a few days later as well. Jim took a Turkish flag and an American flag to the moon, just so he could get permission to show the ark to the world, but he died of a heart attack a few years ago, and never was permitted to climb to the right spot in spite of several attempts. He was given a variety of bureaucratic excuses.

I was very discouraged when I got home from that trip but spent a lot of time thinking about spiritual warfare and Bible prophecy as a result. I became so engrossed in these subjects that I wrote several novels to illuminate some of the more mysterious passages in the Bible.

*Clearly, I believe spiritual warfare is very real
and is usually evident in much more subtle ways
than my encounter in Turkey. The messages of
the media, valueless educational systems, and
insidious addictions may all be the work of
demons in this modern age. Paul admonishes us
in Ephesians to prepare for this battle by "above
all, taking the shield of faith with which you
will be able to quench all the fiery darts of the
wicked one" (6:16).*

—PM

CHARIOTS
OF FIRE

*Let us lay aside every weight, and the sin which so easily
ensnares us, and let us run with endurance the race that
is set before us . . . For consider Him who endured such
hostility from sinners against Himself, lest you become
weary and discouraged in your souls. (Heb. 12:1b, 3)*

My husband, John, is from a small parish outside of
Ballina, Ireland. He grew up in the country on a
cattle farm. Life was simple and routine with a lot
of hard work and a little fun on the side.

Besides running after cattle, his most passionate hobby
was running races. He ran in over a hundred races in high
school, winning almost every one of them. He ran cross-
country, three- and five-thousand-meter races, and the steeplechase. He quickly became the top runner in his home state
and one of the best junior runners in Ireland.

John had just finished final exams at the end of his senior
year in high school when he received a phone call. His teacher

told him there was a Coach Garland on the phone from the United States. At first he thought it was a prank call but quickly realized it was for real. Coach Garland told John that he had a full scholarship for him to the University of North Texas for track and cross-country if he wanted it, but he needed to have an answer right at that moment or the scholarship would be offered to someone else. John had to think fast. He couldn't consult his parents or anything. Something inside him told him to go and that he couldn't give up such an incredible opportunity. Taking a huge blind leap of faith, he told Coach Garland he would take the offer.

Coming to America was no easy task for John. He was coming into a world where he knew no one at all. All the love and support that he always had with him was left behind on the other side of the Atlantic.

It was very difficult for John to leave his family and adapt to a new culture and a new way of life. First, the average temperature in Texas in the summertime is about twenty-five degrees higher than anything he had ever experienced before. It made training for cross-country very difficult. Second, for the first time in his life he had a coach to whom he must answer. In Ireland he had always trained himself. He had to swallow his pride and learn to take some constructive criticism. It was difficult for him to come from a place where he was one of the best athletes to a place were he was just average. He had to work very hard to excel.

After a successful freshman year and a cross-country

conference championship under his belt, John hit a point in his running career that happens to the best of athletes—John went into a huge slump. His running literally fell apart during his sophomore year. His running was so bad that during the spring semester, the coach pulled John into his office and told him that next year his scholarship would be gone. He basically told him that he could either pack his bags and go home or stay and try to win his scholarship back. The coach did leave John with a little light at the end of the tunnel. He told John that if he could place in the top eight at the outdoor conference championships, he could have his scholarship back.

John really struggled to get back on top with his running. He was under so much pressure. I saw him persevere through it all. At the conference championships he fulfilled his coach's requirement to win back his scholarship by placing fourth. He was so elated, but not for long.

When John went to meet the coach about his scholarship, the coach apologized and went back on his word. He had allotted John's scholarship money to another runner from Ireland. He told John that he gave away his scholarship money because he didn't think that John had the ability to finish in the top eight at conference.

John was devastated. He didn't know what to do. He didn't even know if he could afford to stay. John felt like God didn't transplant him from Ireland to America to fail. Despite his current circumstance, he knew God had given him an incredible opportunity and that he needed to follow through with the blessings God had given him. After much consideration, John knew he had to come back fighting.

John decided to stay during the summer, go to school, train, and find a way to earn money for the next school year. Out-of-state tuition was really expensive, and he wasn't quite sure how he was going to manage. Well, the Lord really provided for him. He received an international student grant and his parents were able to help him out a little. Not having to worry about money made it much easier for him to concentrate on his training and school work.

That fall, John renewed his status as a quality runner. At the cross-country conference championships he placed in the top ten and in the outdoor season he won several steeplechase races with personal record times. The coach renewed his scholarship for the next year, and he went on to finish his college career with another cross-country championship and a second place finish at the outdoor conference championships in the spring.

I had never before known anyone who could be knocked down so many times and yet get right back up again. I suppose that was one of the great qualities John had that drew me to him in the first place. I so admired him for his discipline and diligence. The Lord used those troublesome times (and there were so many more) to mold and shape John into the great man he is today.

I am truly blessed to call John my husband. His perseverance through all the different trials he has faced has been a tremendous inspiration to me, and I know it has been to many others. Romans 5:3–4 depicts his outlook on life perfectly. It states, "But we also glory in tribulations, knowing that tribulation produces perseverance; and perseverance, character; and character, hope." He looks back with thankfulness for everything that happened to him during the four years he spent in college.

When facing trials and tribulations, our confidence should rest in knowing that God causes all things to happen for the greater good. Thanks be to God for sending trials that bend our hearts toward Him.

—HG

CHRISTMAS IS . . .

Let them do good, that they be rich in good works, ready to give, willing to share. (1 Tim. 6:18)

I love Christmas. It takes me four days to decorate, and in the years since my kids have left home, I finish before Thanksgiving so we can celebrate longer when they are here for both holidays. I do my shopping all year long, so when September comes, I'm done. Presents are placed under the tree the day it goes up and I give gifts to everyone I see. That is just who I am. One might argue that I'm too caught up in the trappings of decorating or gift giving, but that isn't the attitude of my heart. When I remember why Jesus came, I think what I do to my house or the gifts I give to others demonstrates who Jesus is in my life. Each year I look forward with anticipation to how He wants me to show others the love that came down at Christmas.

I have one dear friend who, several years ago, decided with her husband that instead of decorating for Christmas, they would budget those funds for others. This is the ultimate *What would Jesus do?* attitude—self-sacrifice for the sake of others. Well I, and another friend of mine who also enjoys "presenting" Christmas, decided to decorate their house for them.

A few weeks before Christmas my friend and I, and a third friend, sneaked into this couple's house. (I don't remember how we knew they would be gone or how we got her key!) It was a really cold day and we were so bundled up I was sure any neighbor who saw us thought we were burglars. But then again, what kind of burglars would enter through the front door wrestling a huge tree and carrying in packages?

We had about three hours. Like church mice, we were scurrying around trying to be about our business and having lots of fun. We moved furniture, finally got the tree to stand upright, and had an excess of ornaments to place. All the while we were trying to imagine how our friend would react when she walked in.

We completed our labor of love in time. The house was beautiful. The couple we were doing this for also had three small boys, so we imagined their excitement too. Then probably the best idea concerning this whole adventure occurred to us: *We would never let them know who had done this!* We knew our friend was going to love this and might even think her husband did it but we decided to leave it to speculation.

Laughing, we bundled up our trash and, upon leaving, we surely did look like burglars. But no one saw us. When our friend came home, she called all her neighbors but no one had a clue! (This was before neighborhood crime watch.)

As always, friends dropped by during the holidays and word quickly spread that some unknown persons had decorated her home. At one such gathering, all three "perpetrators" were there. No, we couldn't keep a straight face, but somehow we managed to keep our secret and so it has remained for the last seventeen years! (If by chance she should read this and recognize herself, we love you. And love to my cohorts, Sharon M. and Beverly R.!)

This is what Christmas is. Giving out of love with joy, not for personal glory, just as Jesus did.

At Christmastime and all the time, Jesus wants us to give of ourselves from our hearts. How this manifests itself—giving up decorations, giving decorations, or giving something altogether different—does not really matter. It is the giving that matters.

—BC

Windows
of Opportunity

To everything there is a season,
A time for every purpose under heaven. (Eccl. 3:1)

When my good friend, Doug Franck, with whom I had gone to Russia back in 1993, called me in 1997 and asked me if I wanted to go to Cuba, at first I said that I didn't think so. Getting into the country would be tricky enough, getting out might be even harder. Cuba is still a communist country and fairly unpredictable. Even though I would be going with a team from both Equipping Ministries International and Caring Partners International, I was still hesitant. I did agree to pray about it, however. *What would Jesus do?* You know He would go. And me? Well, after a few days I liked the idea in spite of the risks.

Caring Partners International invited me to join a medical and evangelistic team that would deliver $250,000 worth of badly needed medical equipment to some of the hospitals in Cuba. The group was made up of twenty American doctors, nurses, and an evangelist. We were to be the first medical missions team allowed into Cuba within the last thirty-eight years.

When I arrived at the airport in Cancun to begin my trip, I discovered that the airline had lost my reservations. They said the flight to Cuba was overbooked, as well as the return flight, and I wouldn't be able to go. I decided to wait around until I could board standby. Only a few hours later I was given a ticket. As it turns out, the airline had made a mistake with my ticket, was embarrassed, and ultimately gave me a ticket even though my round-trip flight was overbooked.

My luggage contained about fifty letters from Cuban-American Christians that I was to deliver to their relatives in Cuba. I had placed these letters in a compartment of my luggage. When I arrived in Havana, the guards, as it turned out, searched through all my luggage except for the compartment containing the letters. All I knew was that I was supposed to deliver these to someone named Loraine, who was a Methodist in Havana. A few days later, I spoke at a large Methodist church in that city and asked if there was anyone in the audience named Loraine; there wasn't. After I finished speaking, the pastor invited me to speak to a group of leaders from different denominations who had gathered at a location nearby. It was in that group that I found Loraine Carballo, who turned out to be the head of all the Christian psychologists and counselors in Cuba. Our meeting was definitely by divine providence! She later invited me to return in in a later year to train Christian counselors.

My project during this ten-day visit was to give ten lectures. I would be the first person in thirty-eight years to speak about God in the medical schools of Havana and Cienfuegos. I ended up speaking to more than one thousand doctors and nurses and medical staff, and I was also able to speak to over one hundred communist leaders at banquets. Although I was not allowed to give an altar call, many of the physicians and leaders were in tears when they heard case studies about our New Life Clinic's patients and how turning to Christ changed their lives. Some of these men and women trusted Christ during this week.

We spoke at a Southern Baptist seminary and trained students there. One man had waited nine years to get into seminary and was now in his fourth year. He lived and studied at school during the week and got to see his wife and two children only on weekends. The seminary had only thirty-eight students, with one hundred people on a waiting list. The school needed twenty thousand dollars to admit the additional one hundred students, but this amount was impossible to raise in such an impoverished country. For instance, doctors in Cuba earn only twenty dollars per month, and pastors earn only twelve dollars per month. The reality of their poverty struck me when I bought my new friend, Dr. Victor Gonzales, a forty-five cent Coke; he drank it very slowly, savoring every sip. He said that he was able to buy a soda only once every three to four months. And when he disposed of the can, he was careful to wrap it so that his neighbors wouldn't see the can and be jealous.

The great need in Cuba was overwhelming. I am so thankful, however, that God has opened my eyes and opened my heart to these warm and wonderful people.

Confronted with all this need and opportunity, What would Jesus do and have us do? First, Jesus would have us pray for the spiritual revival and political revolution going on in Cuba. Second, He would have us consider whether or not we should personally get involved in bringing the gospel, or funds, or supplies to this last bastion of communism. Involvement in a communist country, either directly in the country or even at a distance, is a risky proposition. But bringing people to Christ and relief from physical suffering is certainly a pursuit worthy of our time and our efforts.

—PM

Is It That
Big of a Deal?

This is the day the LORD has made;
We will rejoice and be glad in it. (Ps. 118:24)

It was just another one of those days—a Jonah day. I suppose we all get them from time to time, a day with a ton of things to do, both at home and work.

Hurrying to get ready for the day, I, as usual, had my music loudly playing in the bedroom. I was in the bathroom putting on my makeup when I heard a big, loud crash. It was a large crystal picture frame sitting atop one of the stereo speakers. I'm guessing the vibrating bass from the music made it fall, but that's not everything. On its way to the floor, the frame hit my brand new cherry dresser and armoire and put a nice dent in both.

On my way out the door I needed to do some laundry, so I quickly gathered some whites and threw them in. Unknown to me, a red sock went in with it. Later that day, I found my ruined load of clothing.

I rushed out the door and was on my way to work. The phone never ceased to ring. I was dealing with problem after problem and was prevented from finishing what really needed to be done. A crucial shipment I expected in that day was not going to arrive. Responsible for its delivery, I had to get in my car and take a two-hour trip to Greenville, Texas, to pick up our shipment.

On my way, I was on the LBJ freeway, one of the busiest highways in the Dallas metroplex. Out of the thousands of other cars speeding on the freeway that day, the police officer had to pull me over and give me a ticket. I was so annoyed. If that shipment arrived as it should have, I would never have been on that freeway in the first place.

I had so many things go wrong that day, and I didn't get anything finished. By the time I got home, I was in a bad mood. I decided to wind down, so I sat and watched television for a while.

Since there was nothing particularly interesting on television, I found myself channel surfing. In the midst of this mindlessness, I stumbled across a program that deeply convicted me—a fund-raiser for needy children. I watched story after story of children, right here in the United States, who have no clothing, have shacks for shelter, and don't even know where their next meal is coming from. Sometimes these children went days without food.

Suddenly, my day was in perspective. I was thankful that I had a washing machine in which to ruin clothes, I owned nice furniture that could be damaged, and I had a car in which

I could get speeding tickets. Looking back on that day, I wish I had possessed more of a *What would Jesus do?* attitude.

I am learning not to make a big deal out of life's trivial problems. There are many more issues in life that deserve attention—life-and-death issues, issues that have an eternal consequence. So what if my furniture gets damaged or my clothes get ruined? Someone, somewhere, was having a much more terrible day than I. I've known people facing death that have had a better outlook on life than me.

Someday, when my life is ending, all of the possessions and circumstances I got so upset about won't mean anything. My clothes will have been trashed long ago, my furniture will be firewood, my car a hunk of scrap metal, and no one will ever remember whether I got those shipments out on time. The only thing that will matter when it's all said and done, is that I spent my life glorifying the Father in all I did. That includes my attitude when life throws an unexpected curveball.

Live each day knowing that something is bound not to go the way you have planned. You can schedule your life all you want, but you are not the master of the outcome. Consider a What would Jesus do? *attitude the next time you don't*

make it somewhere on time, the washing machine breaks and floods your laundry room, or maybe your spouse didn't do something you asked. Have patience in all things. It not only benefits you, but you shine as an example to others around you.

—HG

Four Days
in Vegas

Yes, and all who desire to live godly in Christ Jesus will suffer persecution. (2 Tim. 3:12)

When my husband and I began our business manufacturing Christian gifts, we researched potential markets for our product. Usually we just went to the markets in which we could afford to participate. One such affordable and convenient show was a college bookstore show in Las Vegas.

The show floor was typical of most conventions, except this was in one of the best hotels on the strip. I think we expected the other exhibitors to have similar products to ours: framed pictures, wood plaques, desk sets, and more, all with inspirational and Scripture messages. Boy, were we mistaken!

As exhibits started going up on our aisle we realized we were really in unfamiliar territory. The vendor's displays immediately around us had neon alcohol advertisements, astrology games, and, the pièce de résistance, an exhibit selling portable showers. A shower was set up with a live model dressed in a flesh-colored body suit demonstrating its "versatility." Men would stand for what seemed like hours gazing upon this apparition.

Before crates were opened as booths went up, participants introduced themselves to each other and joked about the work ahead of us over cups of coffee and with the typical friendly dialogue exchanged among vendors at trade shows. I know my husband told everyone during set-up that we were a Christian gift company, but it wasn't until we started hanging our framed art with Scripture and then finally the sign bearing our name, Christian Craft, that anyone really put it together.

The exhibitors who earlier had been talkative and friendly with us now looked away. There was an invisible barrier that kept them from walking too close to us, and in the last few hours of set-up, when I glanced at any of them, they nervously smiled and avoided eye contact.

My husband and I knew immediately it was the "Christian" in our product name that was making them uncomfortable. I'm sure they were wondering if we were going to preach or point fingers at them. Certainly they were wondering what in the world we were doing in Las Vegas. The next day we were wondering that ourselves.

The day began well enough. Our neighbors around us said a hearty, "Good morning!" even though they left us out of the discussions of "What did you guys do last night?"

The show floor opened and the bookstore managers and

buyers were making their first day walk-through, glancing and sometimes stopping at the exhibits. My husband and I really were not concerned with the early inactivity in our booth until mid-afternoon. Buyers' initial glances would draw them into the booth because of our appealing display and product, but when they realized they were looking at framed Scripture products, they quickly moved on. It was very unsettling. And there wasn't anything we could do about it either.

I stayed within the confines of our booth where I felt secure, but that wasn't my husband's style. Common convention practice is to stop people in the aisles and get them to come into one's booth. My husband was very comfortable doing this, but when he managed to get people in the booth, they quickly left. It really was amazing how Scripture text could intimidate so many people.

By the second day I think the exhibitors around us started feeling sorry for us and wandered over during the lulls to make conversation. We met some other encouraging Christians but they weren't flying their Christianity over their displays. By the third day it was quite obvious that we would probably leave this four-day exhibit without one order.

Always the salesman, my husband went to the pay phones and, with yellow pages in hand, began calling Christian bookstores listed in the Las Vegas area. None of them were even aware that there was a bookstore show going on. Everyone he talked to was quite receptive to the invitation he gave to drop by the exhibits. Finally on the last day of the show, we got some orders from those bookstores that had come to see our line. Their orders paid our expenses.

My husband and I got just a glimpse of what it is to "suffer for Christ's sake." It certainly wasn't physical persecution, but the mental fatigue that was required to constantly stand firm, not only for the sake of our product but for the sake of our personal commitment, was lifted like a weight at the closing day of the show. Although the experience of a four-day trade show seems like something that would fade, the vivid lesson that we learned there was something we have used on many occasions in counseling and in Bible studies as an example of standing firm in faith and commitment.

"My brethren, count it all joy when you fall into various trials, knowing that the testing of your faith produces patience. But let patience have its perfect work, that you may be perfect and complete, lacking nothing. (James 1:2–4)

—BC

The French Lady

Go therefore and make disciples of all the nations,
baptizing them in the name of the Father and of the Son
and of the Holy Spirit. (Matt. 28:19)

In 1992 I went to Israel with Robert Wise, a Jewish believer and a writer who specializes in Jewish novels. Janet Thoma, a vice president at Thomas Nelson Publishers who supervises the production of most of the Minirth Meier New Life books, introduced me to Robert and hired him to help me revise my first novel. We went to Israel in 1992 to verify the details—street names and other facts—of *The Third Millennium*. Later, Robert became the coauthor of my second and third novels.

While in Israel, I decided to visit a messianic synagogue, a synagogue of Jews who observe Jewish customs but have faith in Jesus (Yeshua) as their Messiah and Savior. I slipped in the back row, with the meeting already in progress, and someone handed me earphones so I could hear a translator tell us in English what the rabbi was saying in Hebrew. No one in the church knew me.

The first thing I heard the rabbi say was, "We have lots of problems and persecution here in Israel because we believe in Yeshua. There are no professional Christian counselors here in Israel to help those of us who become depressed or develop panic attacks. So let's all pray that God will send someone, maybe even a Christian psychiatrist from America, to train us how to do specialized counseling." I got goose bumps and felt like I was watching *The Twilight Zone*. I remembered the missionary dream I had when I was sixteen years old and was certain God was calling me to do this. *What would Jesus do* in this "coincidental" circumstance?

I went up to the rabbi after he finished and told him, "Here am I—send me." I teamed up with a former Dallas Theological Seminary student of mine who now teaches in Israel, Ken Hendren, and spent the next four years training about one hundred Jewish and Arabic believers how to do the work of a professional therapist, going back to Israel for one to two weeks annually to train them. My dream was again becoming fulfilled.

In 1993 I took my oldest son, Daniel (a Biola graduate), with me to train counselors in Israel for two weeks. Dan had to leave before me to complete his studies at Biola, so I had to fly home alone. I was shy in high school, but after several years of live radio to over one million people, I had become quite an extrovert. On airplane trips I actually like middle seats so that if one person gets tired of talking to me (or listening to me), I can turn my head and talk to the other one.

On the first leg of my flight home from Tel Aviv, Israel, to Paris, France, no one on either side of me spoke English. I was bored to death. Before getting on the next plane, a twelve-hour flight from Paris to Chicago, I prayed intently, "Lord, please put someone beside me who speaks English." To my pleasant surprise, a lovely, blond-haired, blue-eyed, thirty-year-old woman from Paris sat beside me; and she spoke English fluently. I said a silent prayer, "Thank you, Lord. I'm a happily married man, but she'll do just fine. She'll be fun to talk to. Give me a chance to minister to her on the trip if it's Your will."

We didn't tell each other our names at first, but we began talking and I asked her where she was going. Her reply was "Little Rock, Arkansas." I went to medical school in Little Rock, and it's a very nice city; but I wondered why a Paris native would vacation in Little Rock, so I asked her why she was going there.

"Well," she said, "I have an unusual story, but I'd love to tell you if you don't mind listening."

"I'd love to," I replied.

"Well," she responded, "I lived all my life here in Paris and attended the university in Paris ten years ago. I was engaged, but my fiancé was unfaithful to me; so we broke up and I became deeply depressed. A missionary from Campus Crusade in Little Rock met me, felt compassion for me, and gave me a book titled *Happiness Is A Choice* by Dr. Paul Meier. Have you ever heard of it?"

"Yes, I have," I replied, not yet telling her that I was Paul Meier.

"So I read the book," she continued, "and became a Christian; and now I am a missionary in Lyon, France, with Campus Crusade. I'm going to Little Rock for two reasons: to visit the lady who gave me that book, and also to try and call Dr. Paul Meier; because we have many missionaries here in France but no training in how to counsel many of the tough problems we see, like bulimia, bipolar disorder, and things like that."

"I am Paul Meier," I said matter-of-factly. "When do you want me to come?"

She chuckled but thought I was joking until I showed her my passport. Then she almost fainted. It was another divine appointment—a one in a billion. Ten months later I was in Paris and Lyon, training missionaries how to do Christian counseling (and also counseling the missionaries themselves). My wife and I support that missionary and her husband now.

These two anecdotes illustrate the amazing things that can and do happen when you take the WWJD? *attitude in all areas of life and remain open to God's divine leading.*

—PM

THE DEEPEST
HURT

For Dennis and Jill Windsor
Thank you for sharing your heart.
May you find continued strength through prayer
and hope through healing.

The righteous cry out, and the LORD hears,
And delivers them out of all their troubles.
The LORD is near to those who have a broken heart,
And saves such as have a contrite spirit. (Ps. 34:17–18)

It was the last Saturday evening in October of 1995. We were having a dinner party with our extended family. I remember the ringing phone. Normally, during dinner we would never even answer the phone, but Dad asked me to go into the kitchen and answer it. It was Dennis Windsor, my dad's friend and business partner calling him on his way to the hospital. "Hey, I gotta talk to your dad right now," he said. I just said "OK" and took the phone to my dad.

You could tell immediately that something serious had happened. Anguish came over my dad's face and tears welled up in his eyes. My dad told us what had happened, and he and my mom left immediately for the hospital.

Dennis had just finished up a Spirit-filled weekend at the Promise Keepers rally in Irving, Texas. He was so anxious to go home and be with his family that he left early to help his wife, Jill, and their three children—Daniel, five; Scott, two; and Jessica, five months—get ready to go to the fall festival at their church.

Jill got the boys into their costumes and sent them outside to play while she finished sewing Jessica's costume. She was just seconds away from going outside when their oldest, Daniel, came in to the house and said, "Mommy, I think you better come and see what Scotty did to Daddy's truck."

Her first thought was, "It's Dennis's truck, I'll let him handle it," but Daniel persisted and she raced outside. She saw that the truck had slipped out of gear and rolled down into the creek. She then looked down to the right and saw Scotty lying motionless. She new immediately that he was seriously hurt. It wasn't like Scotty to be so still.

She raced inside to call 911, giving them explicit directions to their house as they live in a remote rural area. After what seemed like an eternity, the paramedics finally arrived. Scotty was in serious condition. They began to work on him right away. The paramedics called for CareFlight, and Scotty was airlifted to Children's Medical Center in Dallas.

It was a long drive to the hospital, over an hour. They didn't know what to expect or what they would find when they got there. On the way, Dennis called in to KCBI radio and asked if they could get a message to the Promise Keepers about what had taken place. During the keynote presentation, thousands of men halted and prayed for Scotty and the Windsors.

Jill remembers arriving at the hospital and being shuttled through what seemed like corridor after corridor. After a few moments she realized where they were being led. A doctor greeted them in a small waiting room with the heart-wrenching words, "I'm sorry, we did all that we could."

I don't think you can even begin to imagine the pain, the devastation, or the disbelief that comes with losing a child, unless perhaps you have been through the same thing. As I write, I'm baffled as I try to share their feelings; I just can't. However, there is someone who can.

What would Jesus do? In the eleventh chapter of John, the author tells the story of the death and resurrection of Lazarus, a dear friend of Christ. We are told that Christ mourned for the loss of His friend. Jesus lived life as a man, He experienced our anguish. He, more than anyone, understands the depths of our hurt. Christ looked to the Father for healing. Whenever Jesus faced trials as a man, His first response was always to cry out to the Father.

As the days and weeks progressed, Dennis and Jill found themselves trying to find a way to deal with their pain. Jill recalls those initial prayers when all she could do was cry out, "God, help!" Jill doubted God's existence and Dennis questioned God's sovereignty. They wrestled with the ever pressing question of why? If God were sovereign over all things, why would he allow all of the mitigating factors that caused Scotty's death to come together at once?

Dennis and Jill renewed their faith and trust in the living God and came to heavily rely on His promises in Scripture. They clung to a few verses like Psalm 33:4 "For the word of the LORD is right; / And all His work is done in truth," and Psalm 34:18, "The LORD is near to those who have a broken heart, / And saves such as have a contrite spirit."

Jill recalls the countless hours they spent reading Scripture and on their knees in prayer. It was their only true comfort. One of their main prayers was that God would allow both of them to grieve together. God answered their prayer. It was through those times of great grief that they were able to grow closer to each other and to the Lord.

What would Jesus do? Friends stopped by each evening to grieve with Dennis and Jill. In the weeks that followed Scott's death, they received over three hundred and fifty letters and cards. Friends would listen as Dennis and Jill read the many cards and letters they received each day. Dennis recalls one card they received with the signatures of fifty families who were praying for them. It was a source of great comfort. They both spoke of how they could literally feel the Holy Spirit's healing touch from all the prayers.

Dennis and Jill recall the first evening they spent alone

after Scotty's death. They had put the kids to bed, got the fireplace going in the living room, and waited for friends to stop in. It was the first night that no one came. They were left feeling so empty. It was then that they realized that friends couldn't keep coming over forever and that God was really the only one who could give the sustaining comfort they so desperately needed.

One thing I have learned from their grief is that you can never fully realize the depth of God's grace, the depth of His understanding, nor the depth of His compassion until your heart has been broken. Today, Dennis and Jill are continuing to place their trust in Christ as they learn the harsh reality of living without their son. The one thing that they have been able to rejoice in is the endurance of God's faithfulness and the gift of peace that the Holy Spirit brings.

What would Jesus do? The fall after Scotty's death, Dennis and Jill decided that they wanted to do something that would honor the memory of their son. After experiencing how difficult the holidays could be during times of great trial, they wanted to do something for the children in their community who would be going through the holiday season with little or nothing to be joyous about. The idea for Scotty's Gifts was born.

Now each Christmas, Dennis and Jill enlist families to adopt underprivileged children in their community and buy necessary clothing and a few toys for the children. Each Christmas Eve they collect and distribute all the presents to the children and share Scotty's story and the wonderful grace of Jesus.

Dennis and Jill continue to be blessed by God's grace. After asking God to grant them one more child, He blessed them with a baby girl. They named her after the verse they continue to cling to the most, "'For I know the thoughts that I think for you, says the LORD, thoughts of peace, and not of evil, to give you a future and a hope," hence Hope Elise Windsor (Jer. 29:11).

Even as a baby, you could see his joy, his buoyant spirit. Scotty loved the outdoors. He loved helping me with housework, riding his bike, swimming in the neighbor's pool . . . And now Scotty is with Jesus, and I'm angry, and I'm hurt, and I want my baby back. But part of me knows that the same hands that so graciously knit that baby together in my womb are now holding him more tightly and tenderly than I ever could. (Jill Windsor, excerpted from Scotty's memorial)

—HG

The Cutting Edge

Therefore by their fruits you will know them. (Matt. 7:20)

The summer between my son's junior and senior year in high school, he and his friend next door started The Cutting Edge lawn service. I think many high school boys enjoy this type of job during the summer because they have more freedom and flexibility with hours, and if they get enough clients, it can be very lucrative. They really were novices at this type of work as both sets of their parents did their own yard work. I could fill pages with comic relief stories about fertilizer striped lawns, postage stamp size yards, and rainy days without work. This story, however, is about a day toward the end of the lawn service season when neither boy was involved.

My son's business partner had gone off to college and most of the boys' clients had decided the growing season was over. Directly behind our own home, however, there were three homes that continued to need service into September. Well, my husband and son had been planning a fishing trip right before school started for quite some time, and the days they planned to be gone were the days my son was scheduled to mow.

I've already mentioned that I do my own yard work. I do it because I enjoy it. So rather than disappoint our neighbors and skip the mowing for that week, I told my son I would do it. The father of my son's partner did one of the yards but had to leave town before he could help with the other two.

For years I have attended Bible study with my dear friend Wendy. Wendy is a servant at heart, and when she found out I was going to mow yards for my son she offered to help.

Of course, I told her it wasn't necessary. The yards were next door to each other and I had often mowed my next door neighbor's yard along with mine and thought it would be a similar task. What I didn't foresee was the grass height and a thunderstorm on its way.

Still, when the day arrived I thought, "No problem." I grabbed my mower and crossed the alley between our home and the first house. After the first few passes across my neighbor's side yard I knew I was in too deep. I had to stop to empty my grass catcher after every other pass. The grass was damp so it made the bag *really heavy*! I have always considered myself strong, but I was tiring quickly. Clouds were churning. The air had turned from hot and sticky to cold and windy and I hadn't even reached the front yard of the first house!

It didn't occur to me to stop. I was, however, glad the

owners of the homes weren't there because they would have been concerned and embarrassed for me. I looked ridiculous and, maybe, too old for the job. Well I finally got to the front yards. I decided to mow both yards at once traversing back and forth. I made a couple of passes wondering if I would finish mowing or just pass out before the storm came when, with perfect timing, Wendy pulled up! She had one of her sons, Chris, with her and they had brought their lawnmower. PTL!

Chris was smiling—he was always smiling. That day I had the feeling he wanted to laugh out loud, but he didn't. He quite effortlessly took the mower from their car and began at the other side of the two yards. Wendy decided she could best help us by being ready to bag the grass. We completed the task like pros, efficiently and expediently, before the storm.

Chris put his equipment back in their car, then Wendy and Chris helped carry the grass bags to the alley for the trash pickup and they helped me get my mower back to my garage. I offered to pay Chris but he said, "No thanks."

Everyone knows Wendy and Chris by their fruit. They always have the heart of service without expecting anything in return. I don't even think they give conscious thought to the promised reward of Colossians 3:23–24, "And whatever you do, do it heartily, as to the Lord and not to men, knowing that from the Lord you will receive the reward of the inheritance; for you serve the Lord Christ." How thankful I am for these dear people willing to take their friendship to The Cutting Edge!

I still am amazed at how silly this whole circumstance was and how much I really needed Wendy and Chris's help. We often think that service for Jesus' sake means witnessing, working at homeless shelters, or raising money for needy causes. Well, it does. But it also means helping our brothers and sisters in little, seemingly unimportant ways. When done heartily for the Lord, all acts of kindness, big or little, are pleasing to God.

—BC

Roots

Having then gifts differing according to the grace that is given to us, let us use them. (Rom. 12:6a)

In a previous story I have told about my parents' childhood in a German community in Russia, then escaping during the communist revolution first to St. Petersburg, then to Germany, and finally to America. Growing up I have always had a fantasy of somehow having a small part in restoring Christianity to Russia, where Satan used communism to try to stamp out Christianity.

In 1993, a few months after my missionary journeys to Israel and France, I received an exciting phone call from Doug Franck with Campus Crusade. Doug asked me if I would be interested in teaching Christian psychology to more than one hundred graduate students of psychology (mostly atheists) at St. Petersburg State University in Russia. Since this was shortly after Yeltsin assumed power in Russia, Doug said the university would now permit me to teach all the Christian principles I felt like teaching. He also told me that students in Russia were curious to hear about Christianity since people went to jail for discussing it just a few months before.

I asked myself *WWJD?* for about ten seconds, then accepted the invitation. A few months later I stood in Russia with Doug and a few Christian businessmen who also came to share their expertise and faith at the university. We first went to Red Square in Moscow where I held up my can of Coca Cola to the Russian soldiers in a toast to Yeltsin. They enjoyed that, and I did too!

Then I met with a handful of Christian psychologists and a Christian psychiatrist in Moscow, encouraging them to boldly integrate their faith into their practice and teaching them techniques on how to do so. I explained to them how we do this at our New Life Clinics in America. Many miraculous things happened on that trip. One time, for example, our paid driver didn't show up, but a complete stranger stopped and took us to the university even though we couldn't speak any Russian and he couldn't speak any English.

I lectured to the students for four or more hours daily, telling them case study after case study of how people's lives were changed through faith in Christ and the application of biblical Christian psychological principles. You could hear a pin drop. Many students wept openly. About half of them trusted Christ as Savior and were followed up on by Campus Crusade. When these new believers graduated, they each went to separate high schools in order to become school psychologists. What a blessing!

The impact of one person asking What would Jesus do? *can have a tremendous ripple effect. Remember that it was two shoe repairmen who preached the gospel and started my Russian ancestors on the path to life in Christ. And now it is I who am able to take this same gospel of Christ back to Russian psychologists who will hopefully spread this message of good news to thousands of Russian school children. And what do I have in common with those two shoe repairmen from years ago? We have taken our individual talents and occupations and used them as a starting place for ministry.*

—PM

Displaced Hearts;
Forgotten Survivors

*I have shown you in every way, by laboring like this, that
you must support the weak. And remember the words of
the Lord Jesus, that He said, "It is more blessed to give
than to receive." (Acts 20:35)*

My mother was born to German parents in
Czechoslovakia in May of 1946, at the close of World
War II. The Stoiber family lived in western
Czechoslovakia in an area commonly known as Bohemia. It
was primarily a German settlement.

After fighting in the Czech army, my grandfather, Franz,
returned home to his family and their quaint little farm on a
hillside outside of Horitz. Even though the Germans in
Bohemia had nothing to do with Hitler's grand scheme, it
wasn't long before the Czechoslovakian people began to display their hatred toward the Germans living in their country.

One day, just a month after my mother was born, Czech
officials came and broke down the front door and told the

family that they must pack their things. They were to be shipped out of the country to West Germany. They were only allowed to take with them what they could carry. They lost their homes, their land, and all their possessions.

The Czechoslovakian army loaded my mother's family, along with thousands of others, onto a train of cattle cars. The families had to reside in those cattle cars for three days before the German government could disperse them into housing. The train my mother's family was on finally came to a stop at a depot near a small farming community named Schambach. The people were all huddled into a local dance hall.

My grandfather had to find a way to take care of his family of five. He was given the name of a family in town who was willing to take on a family of refugees. After a long moment of hesitation, Franz had to swallow his pride and go to the family for help. All kinds of questions and fears flooded over him. How would they receive him? What would they think of this poor dispersed family?

What would Jesus do? A woman of small stature answered the door and invited my grandfather in. To his delight, he was greeted by a hearty smile from Frau Ketterl and her husband. They asked him questions about his family, where they had come from, how many children he had, and how old they were.

Living in a modest house on one acre of land, the Ketterls were not a wealthy family by any means. They had a few farm animals and a garden for food while Herr Ketterl held a very part-time job as the village undertaker. In addition, they had two children of their own to support.

Despite their own circumstances at the end of World War II, Herr and Frau Ketterl displayed great kindness and compassion toward my grandfather and his family. They rearranged their living conditions and offered him the two largest rooms in the house for as long as they needed to stay. For the next eleven years, the Ketterls sacrificed their lifestyle by opening up their hearts and their home to my mother's family.

My mother still reflects fondly on her childhood years that she spent living in the Ketterls' house. She recalls that they could seldom afford to purchase meat because it was hard to find and very expensive. Most of the time the only meat they had was rabbit whenever my grandfather happened to trap one. However, once in awhile, Frau Ketterl would give them some extra pork or chicken meat from their little farm.

My mom talks about how generous Frau Ketterl was. Sometimes she would cook nice big dinners for the family. On occasion, my mom and her sister would go into Frau Ketterl's kitchen and watch her bake just hoping to get a taste. Frau Ketterl always came through with a special treat for them.

My grandparents worked very hard scrimping and saving every cent during that time. After spending those eleven years living with the Ketterls, they were finally able to build a house of their own. They moved to the nearby town of Strasskirchen where the majority of my mom's family resides today.

To this day, my mother so appreciates all that the Ketterl

family did for her family. Without their great love and support, the Stoiber family may not have had the opportunity to get back on their feet again. The Ketterls answered the call of *What would Jesus do?* They sacrificed their home, their possessions, their time, and their lives to give one family a fighting chance. They mastered the art of giving. The Ketterls' kindness was granted from the purest of heart without motive or benefit. "Blessed are the pure in heart, / For they shall see God" (Matt. 5:8).

How many of us today would turn our lives upside down and invite an estranged and displaced family into our home for the next decade? I'd venture to say that kind of sacrifice is rarely experienced anymore. But did Christ do any less for us by allowing his own crucifixion for our sins? This kind of unconditional and monumental generosity isn't just needed after calamity or world wars, it is needed every day. Jesus wants us to give of ourselves and seek out opportunities to help those in need. When we give in this intense way, the blessings we receive in return are beyond measure.

—HG

LITTLE
CHURCH GIRL

*But Jesus said, "Let the little children come to Me, and do
not forbid them; for of such is the kingdom of heaven."
(Matt. 19:14)*

While my father was in the air force, we were stationed in New York, Kansas, and Texas. Throughout my life, I have visited every state except Alaska. Some might refer to me as a "service brat," but my dad went to great lengths to make sure his kids were exceptions to that rule. I think this was because of my mother.

My mother's alcoholism manifested itself long before I was born, but those were the days before people understood drinking could get out of control. I think comments like "heavy drinker" or "she can really hold her liquor" were more common than the label "alcoholic." My mother was so beautiful and added so much life to any party that no one would dare call her a drunk. Even though she did love to party she couldn't tolerate becoming too close to anyone my dad worked with, including wives and children, so we always lived a great distance from the actual air force bases.

My dad was stationed overseas twice during my preschool years. During his absence it wasn't uncommon for the police to find me mosquito bitten and alone in my mother's convertible while she frequented a favorite bar. They would call relatives when we lived near them, or they would take me home. Many times she would take me into the bars where the bartenders would keep "the little girl" content with Shirley Temples or big bowls of maraschino cherries.

My dad stopped drinking when I was four years old because a drunken argument between the two of them ended with Mother missing the first step at the top of the stairs. Her liver burst, last rites were read, and had she died, my dad would have been convicted of manslaughter.

I have often thought if he were living his life today in the same situation, he would be labeled a victim of spouse abuse and considered weak to stay in such an intolerable circumstance. He was a victim, and you may consider him weak, but he never saw himself as a victim. He most definitely was an example of strength in adversity for me, and he demonstrated a love that was sacrificial and unconditional. Was he a believer? He told my husband a short time before his death that if he hadn't been assured of his relationship with Christ, he wouldn't have been able to make it all his years. But did Daddy and I ever talk about his personal relationship with our Lord? Not a word.

If anyone asked, my mother would always say she was Baptist and my dad would say he was Church of Christ. They probably did attend those denominations in their youth, but I never saw them go to church. Which is why I never figured out why Daddy decided to drop me off one Sunday morning at a Methodist church as soon as I reached school age.

Mother would dress me up in pretty dresses, carefully curl my hair into ringlets, and complete the outfit with hat and gloves. Thinking back, I want to imagine she cared about my well-being and this was her way to make up for her other inadequacies. I had a little white leather New Testament, and each Sunday, Daddy would drop me off in time for Sunday school and be waiting when it was over. I didn't actually start going to "big church" until we moved to a town of 328 people and the church was within walking distance.

Perhaps my dad knew I would get affirmation and love from a church body. I definitely felt safe there. I don't remember the adults or kids, but I do remember every Bible story, and in the denomination I was in, the next right of passage as you approached sixth, seventh, or eighth grade, was a comprehensive confirmation class explaining Bible basics before you actually joined the church. The day I walked down the aisle in that tiny congregation to join the church, I was still a little girl alone.

I received my first complete Bible that day. I think I immediately understood it held some key to life.

My dad retired from the service after twenty-two years. He

was in his early forties but the air force wanted him to go overseas again, without his family. He moved us back to Texas near his brother and sister. I was just entering high school. Here I was in a new place with no friends about to become a teenager!

While he was making the decision about what he would do next, my dad leased a house. Guess where the house was? Right across the street from a church in my denomination. I know the Lord's hand was in this. The girls my age that my aunt wanted me to meet attended that church. I went. We immediately became friends, and we're still friends more than thirty years later!

My home life with my mother never changed. She kept a perfect house and had dinner on the table every day when my father got home, but she would start drinking around six each night until she passed out. I never had friends over after school and certainly not to spend the night.

There is no doubt in my mind that had my dad not made the decision to place me in church, my life would probably not be what it is today. My friendship during high school with those girls kept me in that church. I was dating a young man from another denomination that led me to attend his church also. The association with kids in church and godly church leaders was instrumental in getting me to a Billy Graham crusade at age sixteen where it finally all came together for me.

From first grade to my junior year in high school, every moment I was in church brought me closer to that salvation decision. But the person most responsible for where I am today is the father who, for whatever reason, made the decision to put his little girl in church.

Regular church attendance is not a priority for many families today. We lead busy lives and "surely God will understand" if we miss every other Sunday because we need sleep or just can't get it together. Well, maybe God will understand, but if you have children, you must realize how significant this time may be for their future life in the church, as parents themselves, and for their salvation. Children benefit from the Sunday school lessons, certainly; they will probably remember the tune to "Jesus Loves Me" or be able to recite the books of the Bible until their dying day. But they also benefit from a community of Christians who can shower them with love and leave a legacy of positive role models that can carry them through the difficult times that await them in this complex world.

—BC

Miracles

Do not worry about how or what you should speak. For it will be given to you in that hour what you should speak. (Matt. 10:19)

Toward the end of my missionary trip to Russia in 1993, my companion, Doug Franck, and I decided to invite all the older, established psychologists to come and hear me teach for an evening, telling them I was the founder of the largest psychiatric clinic chain in America. We didn't expect many people to show up, since Russians over the age of forty are closed to anything but the atheism they have been steeped in since 1917. We were very disappointed, however, when only one psychologist showed up—a female in her early fifties. Doug and I had paid a twenty-year-old Russian college student to be our interpreter. In that moment, when the *WWJD?* question was implicit between us, we decided we should indeed stay to speak with that one person.

This Russian psychologist told me she wanted to hear what

counseling techniques we used at the successful New Life Clinics in America. "But don't tell me anything about God," she added emphatically. She was a devout atheist and wanted nothing to do with my God.

I asked her if I could practice some of my "insight-oriented" techniques on her, pretending she was my patient, since I would feel funny lecturing to one person. She loved the idea.

I knew from her denial of God and animosity toward Him that she must have had a very distant earthly father and was unconsciously angry toward her father but afraid to admit it to herself. He was probably dead, and since it's taboo to be angry with a dead father, she found it easier to project her "father anger" to the heavenly Father instead and deny His existence. So speculating all these things in my mind, I began guessing some of them with her.

"Was your father gone most of your life?" I asked.

"Why, yes! He was a sailor, and I only saw him for a few days every six months."

"How old were you when he died?

She began to cry at the thought, and replied, "Seventeen."

Then I told her, "When you were seventeen, not only did your father die, but your fantasy died also."

"What fantasy?" she asked me (both of us speaking through the interpreter).

"The fantasy that someday your father would slow down and take the time to have a closer relationship with you. You're angry toward him for never connecting with you, and you probably married someone distant like him to try to fix what went wrong in your childhood."

She wept bitterly and told me she had recently divorced from her distant husband, having finally given up on him ever connecting emotionally.

"You asked me not to mention God," I said softly as I reached out to put my hand on her shoulder. "But can you see now that you have a lot of repressed anger toward your father, and that you have a real void in your life—a father vacuum?"

"Yes," she replied.

"And that you transferred your anger not only toward your husband, but also toward the heavenly Father, thus denying His existence. In fact, you probably also blame yourself in a false guilt/shame sort of way for not being 'good enough' to make your father change careers and come home to spend time with you."

After another wave of open weeping, this Russian psychologist told the interpreter to tell me that this all made sense. She looked down on her lap at the Russian Bible we had given her as a gift when she first arrived, then asked Doug Franck and me a theological question. Then a genuine miracle happened.

Doug began quoting from memory a passage of Scripture that answered her question perfectly. The college student interpreter told it to her sentence by sentence. I remembered memorizing that passage years ago myself. But halfway through the passage, Doug forgot the rest, and I did too. We both had a mental block and glanced at each other in frustration. Then the miracle happened. The interpreter grabbed the Russian

Bible out of the psychologist's lap and opened it, turning no pages, and finished reading the passage to her in Russian.

When he realized what he had just done, he dropped the Bible, trembling, and told us in English what he had just read and asked how he could possibly have done that, since he didn't even know the passage existed. I told him, "God loves her, so God enabled you to do that to show her His love." He explained what I just said to the psychologist and she wept some more, but with a totally new look on her face.

Then she replied in faith while nodding her head up and down, "Not only is there a God, but He has spoken to me tonight."

Imagine what would have happened if we had not done what Jesus surely would have, but instead walked away from this woman. We would have been very polite and apologized, but explained that it was not really worth her time or ours to lecture to only one person. What a tragedy that would have been. We would have missed a spectacular miracle and this precious woman would have missed an opportunity to know God forever.

—PM

TILL DEATH
DO US PART

Walk worthy of the calling with which you were called,
with all lowliness and gentleness, with longsuffering,
bearing with one another in love, endeavoring to keep the
unity of the Spirit in the bond of peace. (Eph. 4:1b–3)

As a Christian today, one of the most terrifying, life-impacting decisions you will ever make is that of marriage. The reason I call it terrifying is because we live in a world where marriage is no longer held sacred. People marry and divorce as often as they buy a new pair of shoes. If one shoe doesn't fit, they figure they can go out and try on a few others. It is this kind of attitude that makes it that much more difficult for Christian marriages to survive today. Not only do we have the influence of our society, but Christians are human. We falter. It's not an excuse, but it happens.

My husband, John, and I have been married for just over a year now, and, like the majority of all newlyweds, we constantly would hear how much we are enjoying married life and each other. Although we have indeed enjoyed married life so far, we both readily admit that we had several concerns entering into this commitment. John was concerned about living up to my expectations, though he never bothered to ask what they were—he just assumed. I think he was relieved to find out, through a little communication, that all I expected of him was to maintain his relationship with the Lord and to be committed to me and his family.

For me, my fears travel further down the road of life. My chief concern has always been how to make love last. I would always ask myself, "What are we going to be like ten, twenty, or thirty years from now? How do we keep the same level of intimacy, not just physically, but mentally?" John and I have had this discussion many times. We made the decision not only to be committed to one another, but we are deeply committed to making our life together a fulfilling one.

So what's next? How are we to go about living our lives in order to protect our relationship from society's influence? And more importantly, how do we increase the depth and fulfillment of our relationship? *What would Jesus do?* Fortunately in Ephesians 5:22–29 we are given a picture of the model Christian marriage.

The passage doesn't tell us that men are masters and women are slaves. It compares the relationship Christ has to the church with the relationship that a husband and wife ought to have with each other. Husbands make their wives' jobs so much easier when they are submissive to the Lord.

A wife will naturally want to respect and revere such. I find nothing more passionate, intimate, and comforting than when my husband and I go to bed at night and he pulls me toward him and says, "Let's say a prayer." It is by far the most touching way one can love and encourage his wife. It goes the same way for wives. If a woman shows respect and adoration for her husband, this will naturally encourage him to want to live up to the standards of being a godly husband in order to maintain the woman's affections.

The apostle Paul writes in Philippians 2:3–5, "Let nothing be done through selfish ambition or conceit, but in lowliness of mind let each esteem others better than himself. Let each of you look out not only for his own interests, but also for the interests of others. Let this mind be in you which was also in Christ Jesus." *WWJD?* Paul tells us that Jesus lived a life of selflessness, humility, and concern for others. These are some of the characteristics of Christ that a great marriage possesses in abundance.

Every day when John comes home from work, no matter what kind of day I have had, I greet him with a big hug and I ask him how his day went. He has told me so many times how comforting that is to him after a stressful day. My goal is to make our home a haven, a place where he can find rest. In turn, usually at lunchtime, he will call me to make sure that my day is going well. That phone call makes me feel so good because I know despite all the things he has to do during the day, he's thinking about me.

So, what about ten, twenty, or thirty years from now? I know that things in our lives are bound to change. We will undoubtedly both change physically, personally, and Lord willing, children will come into the picture. Although children add so much wonder and excitement to our lives, they're enough to turn a household upside down and inside out. In addition, there are many stumbling blocks down the path of life that will interfere with the intimacy of our relationship. There will be times we will not agree and other times when we may do things that hurt one another.

I believe that is why Proverbs 5:18 says, "Rejoice with the wife of your youth." The verse serves as a reminder to us that, even as the years pass and life seems to get in the way, we are to remember and hold to the commitment we made before the Lord to each other. One day at our church, a missionary, Jody Dillow, spoke on relationships. I'll never forget one of the things that he said. He was talking about how so many times couples fight over trivial matters that months and years later they can't recall. Jody said, "One day, when your spouse is on his deathbed, you won't want to remember the hurts, the fights, or the times he didn't do what you expected of him, but you will want to cling to the joys and the wonderful experiences you both shared together. At that point in life, the memories are all you will have left of your relationship, so make it count."

The Lord has numbered the days of every person and, consequently, every couple. A husband and wife may be together for only one day or for sixty years. We should live each day with appreciation for each other, give love as we committed on our wedding day, and create good memories of each day together we are granted. Live with no regrets.

—HG

ABOUT
THE AUTHORS

Beverly Courrege is the author of the runaway bestseller *WWJD: Answers to What Would Jesus Do?*, its accompanying journal, and *WWJD? Think About It.* She is co-owner of Courrege Design, a Christian gift manufacturer. Courrege and her husband, Boo, live in Dallas, Texas.

Paul Meier, M.D., is the cofounder and medical director of the New Life Clinics headquartered in Dallas, Texas. Dr. Meier is also the author or coauthor of more than forty books, including the bestsellers *Love Is a Choice, Love Hunger, The Third Millennium, The Fourth Millennium,* and *Beyond the Millennium.*

Heidi Gardiner is a recent graduate of the University of North Texas. She currently resides with her husband, John, in Garland, Texas. Last fall, she released her first music CD project titled *WWJD* on which she coauthored the title track and "Don't Let the Fire Die." This three-song CD project is available on the internet at

http://www.whatwouldjesusdo.com

or by requesting an order form from

USA Star Productions,
P. O. Box 941493,
Plano, TX 75094.